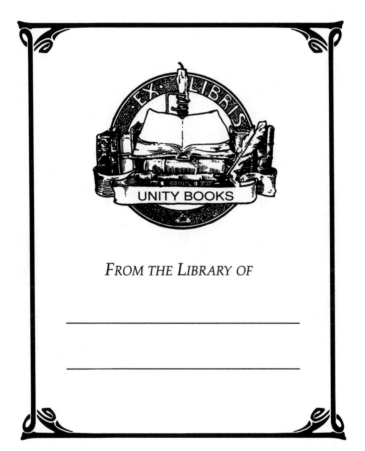

From the Library of

_____

_____

LET THERE BE LIGHT

Also by Elizabeth Sand Turner

Be Ye Transformed
Your Hope of Glory

LET THERE BE LIGHT

THE OLD TESTAMENT
METAPHYSICALLY INTERPRETED

ELIZABETH SAND TURNER

Unity Classic Library

UNITY® Books

Unity Village, Missouri

Let There Be Light is a member of the
Unity Classic Library.

To receive a catalog of all Unity publications (books, cassettes,
and magazines) or to place an order, call the Customer Service
Department: (816) 251-3580 or 1-800-669-0282. For informa-
tion, address Unity Books, Publishers, Unity School of
Christianity, 1901 NW Blue Parkway, Unity Village, MO
64065-0001.

First printing 1954; thirteenth printing 1996

Marbled design by Mimi Schleicher © 1994
Cover design by Jill L. Ziegler

Library of Congress Catalog Card Number: 89-51026
ISBN 0-87159-194-4
Canada GST R132529033

"God always has a blessing for us in every experience, no matter how trying, and we must not let go . . . until we receive it. . . . Our challenge is to hold on until the breaking of day."

Elizabeth Sand Turner

IN MEMORY OF MY MOTHER
ELIZABETH PIERCE SAND
WHO FIRST INSPIRED IN ME A LOVE FOR GOD

FOREWORD

In the beginning God created the heavens and the earth. And the earth was waste and void; and darkness was upon the face of the deep: and the Spirit of God moved upon the face of the waters. And God said, Let there be light: and there was light (Gen. 1:1-3).

These majestic words give the key to the study of the Bible. Our earth, that is, our consciousness is indeed "waste and void" until we know that the Spirit of God within the depths of our being is moving in purposeful activity. Our great need is for light, which represents illumination, intelligence, wisdom. We can have no real comprehension of the Scriptures until we are aware that the Holy Spirit within us is decreeing light.

The Bible was written by men with spiritually illumined minds, and we can understand their words only as divine intelligence illumines our minds. "Let there be light." This command is obeyed as we turn to the divine intelligence active in us. As we accept the light the obscurities of the Bible text are clarified, and a revelation of the supreme truths with which it is replete comes to our eager consciousness.

Whenever we open the Bible we should affirm, "Let there be light," and close it with the grateful acknowledgment, "and there was light." By this affirmation and acknowledgment we attune our minds to the Spirit of truth. Then wisdom scatters the darkness of limited human reason and supplants it with understanding. No longer do we read the Book and find it difficult to understand. With His light shining on its pages the Bible becomes a vibrant, living Word that guides us step by step along the path of spiritual unfoldment.

This book makes no claim to being an exhaustive study of the Old Testament. Rather it aims to give some highlights of the rich spiritual meaning of some of the characters and events, so that he "that runs may read," and he who has the time and the inclination to delve deeper may use this book as a guide.

I have quoted profusely from the writings of Charles Fillmore, for his interpretation of Scripture is the basis of my work as a teacher at Unity School.

The historical data is based principally on "The Abingdon Bible Commentary"; "Essentials of Bible History," by Elmer W. K. Mould; and "The Bible and the Historical Design," by Mabel A. Dominick, Ph.D.

For many centuries the Bible has been a source of instruction and guidance to those seeking light along the way. The seeds of Truth that came to fruitage in the New Testament were sown in the Old Testament, and I doubt whether any seeker of God can fully understand and appreciate the words of the Master without a knowledge of the great teachings contained in the Old Testament. Jesus of Nazareth, the apostles, and Paul were steeped in them; and if we would find "a house not made with hands, eternal, in the heavens" (II Cor. 5:1), we should start with the fundamental idea, "In the beginning God"

(Gen. 1:1). Only by knowing this can we ever enter into the realization of Jesus, "Thou, Father, *art* in me, and I in thee" (John 17:21).

In beginning the study of the spiritual interpretation of the Bible, the words of Origen, an outstanding scholar of Scripture in the third century of the Christian Era, are helpful. He defined the Bible as having a nature similar to that of man, composed of spirit, soul, and body. Charles Fillmore agrees with this. In *Mysteries of Genesis* (page 10) he writes: "As man is a threefold being, spirit, soul, and body, so the Bible is a trinity in unity. It is body as a book of history; soul as a teacher of morals; and spirit as a teacher of the mysteries of being."

Every Truth student should know the historical events recorded in the Bible; he should also be acquainted with its high moral and ethical teaching. The one who would find his way to the "more abundant life" (John 10:10 adapted) must be able to go beyond that and perceive the Bible's spiritual meaning. The writers of the sixty-six books of the Bible penned their words in the spiritual consciousness, and only in the spiritual consciousness can these books be interpreted. The spiritual import of the Bible is the treasure hid in a field; as we dig diligently, more and more of the profound spiritual meaning of the Book is unearthed until we stand awed and grateful to behold its beauty.

There are a few facts that are exceedingly helpful in starting the work of interpretation. Charles Fillmore provides a clue by stating that the Bible is

7

the story of man's generation, his degeneration, and his regeneration. Genesis begins on the high note of the creation of spiritual man, and in its second chapter moves to the activity of spiritual man in forming manifest man. Chapter 3 of Genesis records man's departure from God, known as the "fall of man." From there until the time of Jesus, we view man's efforts in regeneration, his attempt to find the lost Eden. The life of Jesus represents spiritual man in expression, the man each of us is destined to be.

The characters and places in Scripture represent different phases of man's unfoldment. We should project ourselves into the sacred narrative, for only in that way can we see in it our own personal experiences. The Bible is the story of our spiritual growth. It records how we were created, how we lost our divine heritage, and how we may regain it.

The Israelites represent the one who is looking toward God. The heathen tribes stand for various qualities predominant in the sense nature of man. The Israelites were not perfect by any means. Their varied experiences of defeat and victory depict the failure and success of every seeker after God. The effectiveness of their life was measured by their responsiveness to the commands of Jehovah. According to the Bible, no matter how successful the Hebrews were in outer ways, they were considered sinners when they failed to obey the Lord; and no matter if they were in trial outwardly, they received His blessing if they obeyed Him.

The Bible records faithfully what happens when

we are in different states of consciousness. For example, when we begin to perceive something of value in things spiritual but are still largely in sense consciousness, we are likely to try to take the kingdom of heaven by storm instead of being content to progress gradually. The higher teaching is, "precept upon precept . . . line upon line . . . here a little, there a little" (Isa. 28:10). Jacob is a case in point. He was so impatient to receive the benefits of the birthright and blessing that he resorted to dishonest means to secure them. When we try to force an outer advantage before we have earned it, we repeat a trial similar to that which Jacob suffered when he was forced to flee for his life. We have been given the attributes of the Most High in order to express Him, not to get what we want at some particular time. We are often like Jacob was in his early years, when his discernment was only partially developed, and we must go forward as he did, gradually evolving to a higher state of becoming worthy to receive the name Israel, "a prince with God" (*Metaphysical Dictionary, 303*).

In our spiritual development we are sometimes like Daniel, who symbolizes judgment that looks to God for deliverance. At times we are like David, unifying our kingdom of thought and feeling under the impulse of love. Again, we are similar to the apostles, loving Jesus and willing to follow Him but having so little realization of the faith that endures that when a test comes we retreat and have to be instructed all over again. The more personally we can view the Bible story the greater its value is to us.

It is not "flesh and blood" that shows these things to us but our "Father who is in heaven" (Matt. 16:17). We learn the historical facts of Scripture as we learn to read notes in music, but we should not stop there. The fine musician plays not with hands alone but with depths of feeling and understanding. The artist in spiritual things keeps the history of the Bible in the background of his mind to be used whenever necessary; he concentrates his love on its spiritual meaning. Therein are food and drink for all who would know God. He who is growing "in favor with God and men" (Luke 2:52) grows apace on this nourishment until he comprehends something of what Jesus meant when He said, "I am the resurrection, and the life: he that believeth on me, though he die, yet shall he live" (John 11:25, 26).

With reverence and love may you again open your Bible, study it diligently with the hints given in this book, and join with the Psalmist in exclaiming, "O Jehovah, our Lord, how excellent is thy name in all the earth!" (Psalms 8:1).

Elizabeth Sand Turner

PUBLISHER'S NOTE—In this book, Bible references are given in the usual way (Gen. 1:1); references with page number to the *Metaphysical Dictionary* are given (M.D. 23); and references with page number to *Mysteries of Genesis* are given (Mys. of Gen. 10).

Unless otherwise noted, Bible quotations are from the American Standard Version.

10

CONTENTS

CHAPTER I

Allegories of Genesis

Genesis 1 and 2

THE FIRST ELEVEN chapters of Genesis present a number of allegories. The persons and events mentioned were not necessarily actual or real. But the allegories depict supreme spiritual truths that affect all men everywhere. Together with the creation of spiritual man (Genesis 1) and the formation of manifest man (Genesis 2), there are four additional allegories of importance: the fall of man, Cain and Abel, Noah and the Flood, and the Tower of Babel.

Genesis is rightly named, for it is the book of beginnings. From the earliest times man has asked how he came into being. That he was "fearfully and wonderfully made" (Psalms 139:14) is beyond dispute; but who made him and why? All the higher religions of antiquity have speculated on the theory of the origin of man and the universe. Many of these cosmogonies are known to scholars, and even though they differ in particulars, they are sufficiently similar in general outline to suggest a common source. Whether this is the result of a dominant type of cosmological tradition, or whether it grew from man's innate belief that he was created by a superior being, is one of the riddles yet to be solved.

The Hebrews, being closely related to the Babylonians, apparently "borrowed" certain traditions from them and used these as the basis for their own more enlightened conception of God and man. For instance, the 1st chapter of Genesis shows a striking similarity to the Babylonian story of creation as recorded in cuneiform tablets found by archaeologists in 1872 when the library of Ashurbanipal, an Assyrian monarch of the seventh century B.C., was unearthed. While the Babylonian writers believed in many gods and the Hebrews accepted only one god, there are still many likenesses that cannot be attributed to chance. As the 1st chapter of Genesis was written by the priestly school of Hebrew writers after the period of the Babylonian captivity, it is an accepted fact among reputable Bible scholars that the Hebrew narrative had its origin in the Babylonian myth. There was also a Babylonian flood myth that found its way into the Bible in the story of Noah.

These facts in no way lessen the value of Genesis as a spiritual guide. It is evident, however, that to attempt to interpret the allegories literally leads to confusion. The marvel of the Book lies in the profound spiritual insight of the writers who were able to weave allegory, tradition, and folklore into a superb explanation of the great creative law and give in personalized form stories that reveal man's experience in his search for God.

The older account of creation, given in the 2d chapter of Genesis, was the first attempt of Hebrew authors to explain man's origin. Some writer, or perhaps a group of writers, in the middle of the ninth century B.C. wrote this more primitive account that is a part of the "J" or Jehovist document. More than four centuries later, when Hebrew thought had matured spiritually, the magnificent 1st chapter of Genesis was written. Bible authorities generally hold to the belief that there are thus two accounts of the creation of man. Charles Fillmore teaches that the 1st chapter of Genesis records the creation of spiritual man, while the 2d chapter of Genesis records the formation of the soul and body of man. These, with spirit comprise the threefold man.

Spiritual Man

In the opening chapter of Genesis the actor is God, Elohim. "In the beginning God created the heavens and the earth" (Gen. 1:1). Divine Mind creates divine ideas only. These ideas are the foundation of the spiritual universe and constitute the life of spiritual man.

The first command is "Let there be light" (Gen. 1:3). Light is symbolic of illumination, spiritual intelligence, wisdom. "In him [the Logos] was life; and the life was the light of men. And the light shineth in the darkness; and the darkness apprehended it not" (John 1:4, 5). That is, there is light, a creation of Divine Mind, and it is the life of man (embodied in the life force), but, functioning in the mortal consciousness, man is unaware of the wisdom bestowed upon him by his Creator.

The second command is "Let there be a firmament in the midst of the waters" (Gen. 1:6).

Waters represent the "unexpressed possibilities

in mind," says Charles Fillmore (Mys. of Gen. 17).
There must be a firm place in the midst thereof before the mind can unfold and accomplish its mission
of expressing God. The firmament represents the
quality or attribute of faith. Often we think we lack
faith, and then it is well to remember that faith is
an integral part of our being, as God decreed. When
we are distraught and fearful we should declare,
*"Let there be a firmament; let faith come forth to
give stability to my being."*

After each day of creation, "there was evening
and there was morning" (Gen. 1:5). Evening represents completion, and morning represents the activity of ideas. This is the whole secret of progress.
When one step is attained man is ready to go forward. He cannot take all steps at once and should be
content to progress in an orderly, harmonious fash-
ion. The six days represent periods of development
or degrees of mind unfoldment.

The third command is "Let the waters under the
heavens be gathered together unto one place, and let
the dry land appear . . . Let the earth put forth grass
. . . *and* fruit-trees bearing fruit after their kind"
(Gen. 1:9-11).

"The third step in creation is the beginning of
the formative activity of the mind called imagination. This gathers 'the waters . . . together unto one
place' so that the 'dry land' appears. Then the imagination begins a great multiplication of forms and
shapes in the mind" (Mys. of Gen. 18). When the
formative power of mind, imagination, is used

rightly, it imagines or images the perfection of God. As the halt, the lame, and the blind came to Jesus, He imaged the wholeness of Spirit, and "it was so" (Gen. 1:7).

The fourth command is "Let there be lights in the firmament of heaven to divide the day from the night" (Gen. 1:14).

The two great lights represent the faculties of understanding and will, which should function together. Understanding itself is of little value unless it is expressed by the activity of the will, and man's will is a power for good only when it is grounded in understanding.

The fifth command is "Let the waters swarm with swarms of living creatures, and let birds fly above the earth" (Gen. 1:20).

Mysteries of Genesis (page 22) states that the living creatures symbolize the thoughts that swarm in the mind. They are alive and create after their own kind. Birds represent ideas approaching spiritual understanding. They are above earthly thought and carry the mind upward toward the higher realm of Spirit.

The sixth command is "Let the earth bring forth living creatures after their kind, cattle, and creeping things, and beasts of the earth . . . And God said, Let us make man in our image, after our likeness: and let them have dominion over the fish of the sea, and over the birds of the heavens, and over the cattle, and over all the earth, and over every creeping thing that creepeth upon the earth. And God created

man in his own image, in the image of God created
he him" (Gen. 1:24-27).

Charles Fillmore states: " 'Cattle' represent
ideas of strength established in substance. 'Creeping
things' represent ideas of life that are more subtle
in their expression, approaching closer to the realm
of sense. . . . The 'beasts' stand for the free energies
of life that relate themselves to sensation" (Mys. of
Gen. 24).

The man here referred to as made in the image
and likeness of God is spiritual man, the perfect
idea of man in Divine Mind. Spiritual man is called
Lord or Jehovah in the Old Testament and Christ in
the New Testament. This is the spiritual or higher
nature of all men. In his spiritual self man has dominion over every idea coming forth from Divine
Mind. "The sixth step in creation is the concentration, in man, of all the ideas of Divine Mind" (Mys.
of Gen. 28).

"And God saw everything that he had made,
and, behold, it was very good" (Gen. 1:31).

God is the sole creator, and His creation is good.
There is no evil in His work; therefore evil has no
enduring reality. Our true being is divine and perfect, and as we establish this idea in consciousness
and discipline the mind to acknowledge it, we are
in tune or harmony with God, the source of all our
good.

The first three verses of the 2d chapter of Genesis
actually belong to Chapter 1. God "rested on the
seventh day from all his work which he had made."

This is the Sabbath, the rest of God after the six steps or mind movements called days, in which the spiritual universe and spiritual man are brought forth. "He has created the ideas or patterns of the formed universe that is to follow" (Mys. of Gen. 28).

Manifest Man

Beginning with Genesis 2:4, Jehovah God executes what Elohim God created or ideated. The Scofield Reference Bible (page 6) gives an enlightening definition of Jehovah:

"The primary meaning of the name LORD (Jehovah) is 'the self-existent One.' . . . But *Havah,* from which Jehovah, or *Yahwe,* is formed, signifies also 'to become,' that is, to become known, thus pointing to a continuous and increasing self-revelation. Combining these meanings of *Havah,* we arrive at the meaning of the name Jehovah. He is 'the self-existent One who reveals Himself.' "

Jehovah represents spiritual man from which soul and body are derived. "And Jehovah God formed man of the dust of the ground, and breathed into his nostrils the breath of life; and man became a living soul" (Gen. 2:7).

Spiritual man (Jehovah), being the creation of Divine Mind, is perfect and that to which he gives life is likewise perfect. True it is that the soul has gone astray, looking to the outer for guidance instead of to the inner. However, it is necessary to remember that the soul, which is the self-conscious-

ness, is spiritual in origin and can and must learn
to express the reality of its existence. It is a "living
soul"; that is, it partakes of the life of God; so also
does the body partake of the divine life.

The "dust" from which the body was formed
represents radiant substance. "When spiritual man
(I AM) enters into this 'dust of the ground' (substance) and makes use of the God ideas inherent
in him, he brings forth the ideal body in its elemental
perfection. The real body of man is not material
but is of the nature of the universal-dust body,
which is the divine-substance body. Therefore the
perfect image-and-likeness man is perfect in body
as well as in mind" (Mys. of Gen. 33).

It is the "divine substance" body that is "a temple
of the living God" (II Cor. 6:16). Paul says plainly,
"There is also a spiritual *body*" (I Cor. 15:44).
The basis of all manifest form is a spiritual idea.
When man discerns the spiritual embodied within
the form, he is strengthened and renewed in mind
and body. In such discernment is the key to spiritual
healing.

"And Jehovah God planted a garden eastward,
in Eden; and there he put the man whom he had
formed" (Gen. 2:8).

Charles Fillmore defines the Garden of Eden
as, "a concentration, in man, of all the ideas of God
concerned in the process of unfolding man's soul
and body. When man is expressing the ideas of Divine Mind, bringing forth the qualities of Being in
divine order, he dwells in Eden, a state of bliss, in a

harmonious, productive consciousness containing all possibilities of growth" (Mys. of Gen. 35).

The man whom Jehovah formed is called Adam. The name Adam means in Hebrew, "a human being," and represents humanity as a species. Charles Fillmore terms Adam "generic man" and states that spiritually he represents "the first movement of mind in its contact with life and substance" (M.D. 23). Adam is placed in the Garden to "dress it and to keep it" (Gen. 2:15); that is, he is to care for and express the pure ideas of Divine Mind. That is man's highest and noblest service. He is permitted to eat of every tree in the Garden except the tree of the knowledge of good and evil, but in the day that he eats of that tree he shall surely die (Gen. 2:17). This is the command to man not to appropriate (eat) ideas relating to sensation without proper control. "When man controls his feelings and emotions his sensations are harmonized and all his functions are supplied with nerve energy" (Mys. of Gen. 36). In eating of the forbidden fruit, that is, succumbing to the enticements of the sense consciousness, man brings disaster upon himself.

All the beasts of the field and birds of the heavens are brought to Adam, who is given authority to name them. "Whatever we recognize a thing to be, that it becomes to us because of the naming power vested in man" (Mys. of Gen. 40). The beasts and birds represent ideas moving in mind, and whatever Adam recognizes or calls them, that is what they become to him. In man's power to name or identify states of consciousness outpictured as conditions in his life lies his ability to gain control over them.

In our Scripture narrative we are told that Adam needs a helpmeet, and Eve (woman) is formed by Jehovah God. "Adam is the objective and Eve the subjective in primal man, both in the same body. As man evolves Eve becomes objective. 'This is now bone of my bones and flesh of my flesh: she shall be called Woman, because she was taken out of man'" (Mys. of Gen. 42). Man represents the active side of Being and woman the passive. The masculine quality of wisdom should be joined with the feminine quality of love.

"If the ego or will that is man has adhered to the guiding light of Spirit faithfully and has carried out in its work the plans that are ideated in wisdom, it has created a harmonious consciousness. The original Adam in Eden is symbolical of such a consciousness" (Mys. of Gen. 42).

CHAPTER II

Additional Allegories of Genesis

Genesis 3-11

TOGETHER WITH the allegories recorded in Genesis 1 and 2, the following four—fall of man, Cain and Abel, Noah and the Flood, and the Tower of Babel—tell how man lost an awareness of his divine heritage, of his experience in functioning apart from God, and of his efforts to reach toward Him.

Fall of Man—Genesis 3

There is a question in the mind of man as to why, being created a spiritual being after the image and likeness of God, he should know limitation. The 3d chapter of Genesis purports to answer this by relating how Adam and Eve disobeyed God and were driven from the Garden of Eden. In the Garden they were given all they could desire or need, but Jehovah God commanded them not to eat of the tree of the knowledge of good and evil, adding, "for in the day that thou eatest thereof thou shalt surely die" (Gen. 2:17). Man cannot live to himself alone. He must function in harmony with Jehovah God, which makes it mandatory that he obey certain divine laws. These are made known to him when he listens to the Lord. However, like his Creator, man has free will and, therefore, must decide for himself alone whether he will hearken to the inner voice of Spirit or yield to the outer voice of the serpent.

Charles Fillmore states that the serpent represents the sense consciousness. "It may also be called desire, sensation, or the activity of life in external manifestation apart from the divine source of life" (Mys. of Gen. 49). We are all subject to temptations presented by the sense consciousness. They come not once but daily and find a vulnerable spot in the feeling nature (Eve). Thus the serpent addressed Eve:

> Yea, hath God said, Ye shall not eat of any tree of the garden? And the woman said unto the serpent, Of the fruit of the trees of the garden we may eat: but of the fruit of the tree which is in the midst of the garden, God hath said, Ye shall not eat of it, neither shall ye touch it, lest ye die. And the serpent said unto the woman, Ye shall not surely die: for God doth know that in the day ye eat thereof, then your eyes shall be opened, and ye shall be as God, knowing good and evil. And when the woman saw that the tree was good for food, and that it was a delight to the eyes, and that the tree was to be desired to make one wise, she took of the fruit thereof, and did eat; and she gave also unto her husband with her; and he did eat (Gen. 3:1-6).

The cardinal sin is eating of the forbidden fruit and knowing good and evil. "If therefore thine eye be single, thy whole body shall be full of light" (Matt. 6:22), said Jesus. Knowing good only is necessary if we are to express good only. When we are disobedient to the divine command and appropriate the fruit of evil, it will inevitably come into manifestation. Why do we yield to the Tempter? The answer is that what is offered appeals to the appetite, the sensuous nature, and the desire for worldly wisdom.

Scripture states that "the serpent was more subtle than any beast of the field which Jehovah God had made" (Gen. 3:1). The temptations of the carnal nature are ingenious indeed. We think we can pamper this, that, and the other appetite and "get by with it." "Ye shall not surely die," said the serpent, implying that God does not mean what He says; that we can break His law and not suffer the consequences. It was as if the serpent had said, "Come, this is pleasant, and you'll enjoy it." So, like Eve, we eat. Moreover, Eve gave the fruit to Adam, and he did eat.

Then the day of reckoning comes. When Adam and Eve heard the voice of Jehovah God they hid themselves, for, said Adam, "I was afraid, because I was naked" (Gen. 3:10). He was afraid because he was unclothed, unprotected. In obedience to God there is no fear, but in disobedience, fear is born.

The Adamic Covenant, the second of the eight covenants in the Bible, conditions the life of the fallen man. The judgment for disobedience to divine law is severe indeed. First the serpent is cursed: "Upon thy belly shalt thou go, and dust shalt thou eat all the days of thy life" (Gen. 3:14). The sense consciousness (the serpent) is ever the cause of man's downfall. To Adam the verdict was, "cursed is the ground for thy sake; in toil shalt thou eat of it all the days of thy life . . . in the sweat of thy face shalt thou eat bread" (Gen. 3:17, 19). To Eve, Je-

hovah God said, "I will greatly multiply thy pain
. . . thy desire shall be to thy husband, and he shall
rule over thee" (Gen. 3:16). Death was the final
penalty: "For dust thou art, and unto dust shalt
thou return" (Gen. 3:19).

Man's disobedience to divine law is the underlying cause of his suffering. God provides all good
for him, but he brings labor, pain, and death upon
himself. The tree of life, which is in the midst of
the Garden and of which he should eat, is guarded
by the Cherubim and a "flame of a sword which
turned every way, to keep the way of the tree of life"
(Gen. 3:24). In his fallen state man cannot eat of
this tree.

> Who shall ascend into the hill of Jehovah?
> And who shall stand in his holy place?
> He that hath clean hands and a pure heart;
> Who hath not lifted up his soul unto falsehood,
> And hath not sworn deceitfully
>
> (Psalms 24:3, 4).

All great spiritual teachers insist that we must be
righteous, and they tell us how to attain righteousness. In The Revelation of John, John sees man
again eating of the tree of life whose leaves are "for
the healing of the nations" (Rev. 22:2).

Cain and Abel—Genesis 4

The name Cain means "possession" and refers to
the quality in the consciousness that works to acquire or possess selfishly (M.D. 135). Cain was
a tiller of the soil, which implies that he belonged

to the earthly realm. Abel means "breath," which connects him with the spiritual plane (M.D. 12).

Cain and Abel were brothers, showing that these qualities are often closely related in consciousness. The story goes that each brought offerings to Jehovah, who accepted the offering of Abel but rejected that of Cain. This means that when the consciousness is permeated with spiritual ideas it is closer to the divine, more acceptable to Jehovah than when it is filled with material or worldly thoughts. Cain, in anger, slew his brother. This represents the overcoming of the spiritual by the carnal nature, which happens frequently in our own experience when our spiritual impulses (Abel) are overthrown by jealousy, anger, and selfishness (Cain).

When the consciousness is dominated by its lower self, which is a violation of divine law, one meets hardships. Jehovah said to Cain, "Cursed art thou . . . when thou tillest the ground, it shall not henceforth yield unto thee its strength; a fugitive and a wanderer shalt thou be in the earth" (Gen. 4:11, 12). And Cain cried, "My punishment is greater than I can bear" (Gen. 4:13). When we are disobedient to the spiritual law of our being, we bring negative conditions into our lives and sometimes we feel that they are more than we can bear. We, too, go and dwell in the land of Nod. Nod means "wandering with uncertainty" (M.D. 488) and represents the bewilderment and confusion of man when he loses contact with the spiritual self.

But another son was born to Adam and Eve to take the place of Abel. His name was Seth, which means "compensation" or "substituted" (M.D. 584). The spiritual (Abel) may be overcome temporarily by the mortal thought (Cain) but it will rise again, as is symbolized by the birth of Seth. It is the undying, eternal part of us that will always reassert itself. Seth therefore represents man's spiritual development. His first famous descendant was Enoch. "And Enoch walked with God: and he was not; for God took him" (Gen. 5:24). One who walks with God does not meet the common experiences of those in lower states of consciousness. He is lifted into the spiritual realm. "Enoch represents entrance into and instruction in the new life in Christ" (Mys. of Gen. 69). Enoch's son was Methuselah, whose life span is the record, 969 years! Methuselah was the grandfather of our next outstanding character, Noah.

Noah and the Flood—Genesis 6-9

"And Jehovah saw that the wickedness of man was great in the earth, and that every imagination of the thoughts of his heart was only evil continually" (Gen. 6:5).

When men sin they draw evil to themselves. The Lord (the law) brings back to them what they give forth. Noah was the only man who found grace in the eyes of the Lord, for he was just and righteous. He, too, "walked with God" (Gen. 6:9) and was preserved. The name Noah means "rest,

calm, peace" (M.D. 486). When one is at peace
with his Lord he is protected.

Noah was instructed to build an ark into which
he and his wife and his three sons and their wives,
together with two of every living creature, were
to retire during the Flood that was to cover the earth.
Charles Fillmore says, "The ark represents a positive, saving state of consciousness, which agrees
with or forms a covenant with the principle of Being" (Mys. of Gen. 77). This consciousness is built
when we rest in God and seek to do His will. The
practical lesson to be derived from Noah and the
Flood is that, regardless of how destructive are
the conditions surrounding us, if we are in tune
with the Spirit of truth indwelling we shall be saved
from the devastation that overwhelms those in negative states of mind. We are commanded to build an
ark, that is, to abide in the realization of the one
Presence and one Power. The idea is brought out in
the 91st Psalm where the promise is made to the one
who dwells in "the secret place of the Most High":

> A thousand shall fall at thy side,
> And ten thousand at thy right hand;
> *But* it shall not come nigh thee
> (Psalms 91:7).

We should not be afraid when dread conditions
appear. We can go into the ark that we have built
with many declarations of Truth, and there we shall
be safe.

It rained forty days and forty nights, and the
ark rested safely on Mount Ararat. This means that

trial continued for a period of time but the ones in the ark (realizing the abiding presence of God) were safe.

After the storm abated, Noah sent forth a dove three times; when she did not return on the third occasion, he removed the covering from the ark and saw that the ground was dry. Those in the ark went forth, and Noah built an altar to Jehovah and offered sacrifices. "The altar in this case represents an abiding resolution of the spiritual-minded one (Noah) who makes a covenant with the Lord to continue to 'sacrifice' his sensations or transmute them on the spiritual plane" (Mys. of Gen. 84). We should do this when we have been protected through a great trial.

Noah had three sons: Shem (renowned), who represents the spiritual; Ham (hot), who represents the physical; and Japheth (extended), who stands for the intellect or reason. The greatest was Shem, and through him the spiritual consciousness was continued. Noah's commands regarding his sons are significant:

> Blessed be Jehovah, the God of Shem;
> And let Canaan be his servant
> > (Gen. 9:26).

That is, let the flesh (Canaan or Ham) come under the dominion of the spiritual man (Shem).

> God enlarge Japheth,
> And let him dwell in the tents of Shem;
> And let Canaan be his servant
> > (Gen. 9:27).

That is, let the intellectual man dwell under the protection of spiritual man, not as a servant but as a younger brother. This physical man (Ham) comes under the dominion of both intellectual and spiritual man.

The Tower of Babel—Genesis 11

The final allegory is the Tower of Babel. The descendants of Noah eventually became very ambitious and built a city and then began to build a tower that they hoped would reach to heaven. Their idea was a material one, for they built with bricks and mortar (symbols of the material), and their project was therefore doomed to failure. One does not reach heaven by material means, no matter how clever he may be.

There is a connection between earth and heaven. The ladder that Jacob saw symbolizes the relation between the inner spiritual realm and the outer plane of manifestation. The Tower of Babel, however, is symbolic of man's effort to work without God. The name itself means "confusion" (M.D. 92), and "represents the mental chaos that is the result of thinking from a wholly material standpoint" (Mys. of Gen. 109).

The Lord (the law) confused the speech of the people so that they no longer understood one another, and He did "scatter them abroad upon the face of all the earth" (Gen. 11:9). Men fight because they do not understand one another; they have divers interests, and each pursues his own selfish ends. The Tower of Babel stands for self-service. The spiritual dictum is, "The Son of man came not to be ministered unto, but to minister" (Matt. 20:28). Self-service leads to confusion and the scattering of man's forces. Service to God and to others enables man to speak in the tongue all know as their own. This the apostles did after being endued with power from on high at Pentecost.

CHAPTER III

Abraham

Genesis 12-26

W ITH THE 12th chapter of Genesis, Hebrew history begins. The family of Abraham belonged to one of the Semitic tribes that migrated to the neighborhood of Ur in the south of Mesopotamia. Their kinsmen of ancient times were the Babylonians, Assyrians, Aramaeans, and Phoenicians. The founders of three world religions were Semites: Moses, Jesus, and Mohammed. Abraham is known as the "Father of the Hebrews," for it was under his leadership that a group separated itself from other Semitic tribes and settled in Canaan. The Bible refers to their descendants as Hebrews, which was their racial name; Israelites, which was their religious name; and Jews, which was the name given them about the time of the Babylonian captivity, when all the Hebrews were from Judah.

Metaphysically, Abraham represents the first step in the redemption of man from mortal to spiritual consciousness. He symbolizes faith, not the full and complete expression of that quality, but rather the beginning of faith that is willing to follow the guidance of the Lord and go forth into a new land, symbolic of a new consciousness.

In the beginning of the story of Abraham, he is called Abram and his wife Sarah is called Sarai.

Their names were later changed by the Lord to the more familiar forms. Abram's father Terah was prompted to go to Canaan and moved from the south of Babylonia to Haran. The name Terah means "loitering" (M.D. 651), which signifies that man loiters or delays until faith takes a hand. Have you ever felt the spiritual prompting to go forward but hesitated so long that the inspiration left you? Terah died in Haran, as we "die" when we do not obey the divine urge.

Abram was seventy-five years of age when the Lord spoke to him, which implies that man is mature in understanding before he is aware of spiritual direction.

Now Jehovah said unto Abram, Get thee out of thy country, and from thy kindred, and from thy father's house, unto the land that I will show thee: and I will make of thee a great nation, and I will bless thee, and make thy name great; and be thou a blessing . . . and in thee shall all the families of the earth be blessed (Gen. 12:1-3).

If we aspire to go to a new land (higher realization of Truth), we must be willing to leave the old. Though we wish to enter into better experiences ofttimes we are reluctant to relinquish what we are now enjoying. "Choose you this day whom ye will serve" (Josh. 24:15). Many would like to have the blessings of the spiritual kingdom and still retain the mortal consciousness. That is impossible, however; we must make a choice.

When we have attained the Abram state of

realization—that is, when our faith in God is quickened—we realize two spiritual truths. The first is
that He wishes us to move into a new land, symbolic of a better consciousness.

"Get thee out of thy country" (Gen. 12:1), is
the command when we are prepared to progress. In
coming into a higher state of consciousness we must
relinquish many of the beliefs that belong to mortal
mind. Spiritual realization demands an entirely new
viewpoint on everything: God, ourselves, our environment, our destiny. In our former belief, God
was a superman, and we were mortal creatures made
of flesh and blood only. Our environment was inflicted upon us, and our destiny—heaven or hell.
These beliefs must go, for in this more enlightened
way of thinking we behold God as the creative life
and ourselves as His offspring, made in His image,
and with the responsibility of expressing the attributes we inherit from our divine parent.

Our environment is of our own making, a true
picture of our state of consciousness. Since we make
the conditions of our lives, we can change them. Our
destiny is heaven, not a place of bliss to which we
go after death but a consciousness of oneness with
God. This comes to each man when he is disciplined,
purified, and lifted by God's grace and his own effort. While this is a happier viewpoint, it is also
one that is more difficult to assume, for the responsibility of growth and unfoldment is placed upon the
individual. It deprives him of all excuses for deficiencies. We are glad for the illumination afforded

by Truth when it first comes to us: we feel like new
creatures and are eager to enter the new land. Then
when we are called upon to surrender the error
habits we have acquired, which are adverse to our
spiritual nature, when we know we have to discard
destructive attitudes of mind, such as prejudice and
resistance, we are prone to take on the Terah characteristic of loitering. But, having heard the call
with the Abram faculty of faith, go forward we
must.

The second realization that comes when faith is
quickened is that God has blessings in store for us;
"I will make of thee a great nation, and I will bless
thee, and make thy name great; and be thou a
blessing" (Gen. 12:2). God wishes to give us infinite good. Did not Jesus say, "Fear not, little flock;
for it is your Father's good pleasure to give you the
kingdom" (Luke 12:32)? Our lack is not due to divine intent but to our inability to accept what the
Father has prepared. This great promise is con-
tingent upon our entering a higher state of consciousness (the new land). The expression of His
will is, "I will bless thee." Not only that, but as we
receive from the Father we give and thus become a
blessing to others. "Be thou a blessing" (Gen. 12:2).

These two realizations—that God desires to lead
us into a higher consciousness, and that He wishes
to bless us—are fundamental to spiritual unfoldment.

And Abram took Sarai his wife, and Lot his brother's
son, and all their substance that they had gathered, and

the souls that they had gotten in Haran; and they went forth to go into the land of Canaan; and into the land of Canaan they came (Gen. 12:5).

Sarai went with Abram. Women represent the feeling nature that is ever a part of man's being. Lot likewise accompanied Abram. The name Lot means "hidden or concealed" (M.D. 405) and stands for the negative side of faith, that is, faith in material things. Even though faith in God has been quickened, we still have a residue of faith in material things. We have to be separated from this negative faith as Abram was later separated from Lot.

The events of Abram's life give a true picture of our efforts to sustain faith in God. While Abram had sufficient faith to heed the Lord's command, he faltered on several occasions. Faith has to be rooted in principle, and no one grasps principle in the twinkling of an eye. So, when there was a famine in Canaan, Abram went to Egypt. Egypt represents the sense consciousness to which we are apt to retreat when things go awry. Sometimes it is difficult to meet a trying situation in the spiritual consciousness; it seems easier to handle things in the material way, and (metaphysically) we go down into Egypt.

Abram hoped for good treatment at the hands of the Egyptians and, thinking that a beautiful sister might increase his chances of favor, he passed Sarai off as his sister. This was a half-truth for Sarai was Abram's half sister, but she was also his wife. Frequently a half-truth is worse than an outright falsehood, and so it proved in this particular instance.

Sarai was taken to the house of Pharaoh, "And Jehovah plagued Pharaoh and his house with great plagues because of Sarai, Abram's wife" (Gen. 12:17). The material (Pharaoh) and the spiritual (Abram) states of mind are not compatible, and when we try to mix them the outcome is never advantageous. Perhaps that is the reason why we still have trials even though we are endeavoring to live by spiritual standards. We have gone too far to give up the spiritual but are afraid to go "all the way" with it. We mix in the mortal, or try to, and the result is a house divided against itself. Abram was ordered out of Egypt: the sense consciousness would be rid of the spiritual. The man of Gadara, possessed of demons, cried out to Jesus: "What have I to do with thee, Jesus, thou Son of the Most High God? I adjure thee by God, torment me not" (Mark 5:7).

After Abram returned to Canaan he became a rich man, symbolic of the increasing power of faith. He and Lot had so many herds that the land was not able to support them, and their herdsmen quarreled over pasture rights. Though Abram was the leader of the Hebrews and could have asserted his authority, he proved his generosity by suggesting to Lot that they separate, and he gave Lot his choice of the land. Lot (faith in material things) chose the most fertile section, the plain around Sodom and Gomorrah. To Abram was left the hilly country near Hebron. For a time it looked as if Abram had

lost by his generous gesture, but the Lord said to
him:

> Lift up now thine eyes, and look from the place where
> thou art, northward and southward and eastward and west-
> ward: for all the land which thou seest, to thee will I
> give it (Gen. 13:14, 15).

It is from the "hill," or the high place in consciousness, that we get a grander view of life and
all that it holds, and God always gives to us in accordance with our own ability to perceive. "Seeing"
or recognizing our good is the first step in demonstration. When we see from the heights, our blessing is greater than we hoped for: "all the land which
thou seest, to thee will I give it."

No one who is grossly selfish succeeds for long,
and Lot soon ran into trouble. The neighboring
tribes made war upon Sodom and Gomorrah, and
Lot and all his household were taken captive. One
of his servants escaped and went to Abram for assistance. Abram gathered together his fighting men
and hastened to the rescue of Lot. His men fell upon
the enemy unexpectedly at night, and the enemy
fled, leaving behind all they had. On his journey
home Abram met two kings, one of whom, the
king of Sodom, was so grateful to Abram for having liberated his city that he offered to divide the
spoils of battle with Abram. Abram declined and
gave the king of Sodom all the people and the
goods that had been taken. The other king was
Melchizedek, king of Salem. He brought forth bread

and wine and blessed Abram, for Melchizedek also worshiped God. To Melchizedek Abram gave a tenth of all that he had. "Melchizedek really refers to the Christ Mind or superconsciousness, that which when ruling in man's consciousness establishes and maintains right doing, perfect adjustment, peace, and perfection" (M.D. 438).

Later when Abram was warned that Sodom and Gomorrah were to be destroyed because of the wickedness of their inhabitants, he prayed that the cities be forgiven. However, there were not even ten righteous men therein, and their doom was sealed. Only Lot, his wife, and his daughters escaped. Lot's wife did not benefit by it; she "looked back" (Gen. 19:26) and became a pillar of salt. When one is freed from a difficulty it is disastrous to look back. Jesus said, "Leave the dead to bury their own dead" (Matt. 8:22).

Abram and Sarai were childless, and more than anything else Abram wanted a son to carry on God's mission for the Hebrews. The Lord had promised them a son, but they grew impatient for the fulfillment of the promise. At Sarai's suggestion, Abram took her Egyptian handmaid Hagar as a wife. Ishmael was the child of this union, but he was not the son of God's promise. We should learn to rest in the Lord and wait patiently for Him. Whenever we attempt to force our good the result is unsatisfactory. Abram realized this and waited for word from the Lord. This word was: "My covenant is with thee, and thou shalt be the father of a multitude of nations. Neither shall thy name any more be called Abram, but thy name shall be Abraham; for the father of a multitude of nations have I made thee" (Gen. 17:4, 5).

"The change in name always denotes a change in character so pronounced that the old name will no longer apply to the new person. . . . The new name, Abraham, 'father of a multitude,' when we apply it individually means that our faith is to be expressed by bringing the multitude of our thoughts into the realm of Spirit and under the guidance of the Christ" (Mys. of Gen. 151).

At this time Sarai's name was also changed, for the Lord said to Abraham, "As for Sarai thy wife, thou shalt not call her name Sarai, but Sarah shall her name be. And I will bless her, and moreover I will give thee a son of her . . . and she shall be *a mother of* nations; kings of peoples shall be of her" (Gen. 17:15, 16).

The name Sarai means "bitter" or "contentious," while Sarah means "noble woman" (M.D. 573).

In spiritual symbology woman represents the soul or intuitive part of man. Sarah is the higher phase of the soul. In Sarai the soul is contending for its rightful place in consciousness; the individual is just recognizing the fact that his affections and emotions are in essence divine and must not be united with material conditions but with Spirit. In Sarah this is more fully realized and expressed (Mys. of Gen. 155).

To the human sense the promise seemed impossible of fulfillment, as Sarah was old, but Abraham "believed in Jehovah; and he reckoned it to him for righteousness" (Gen. 15:6). Often it seems as if there is no way for our prayer to be answered. This is because we see with limited vision, and God requires that we trust Him to show us the way.

The son born to Abraham and Sarah was named Isaac. The name means "laughter," or "joy" (M.D. 299). This joyous quality (Isaac) is the child or off-spring of faith (Abraham) (M.D. 17) and intuition (Sarah) (M.D. 573). Some years later a test came to Abraham as regards this son that the Lord had given him.

And it came to pass after these things, that God did prove Abraham, and said unto him, Abraham; and he said, Here am I. And he said, Take now thy son, thine only son, whom thou lovest, even Isaac, and get thee into the land of Moriah; and offer him there for a burnt-offering upon one of the mountains which I will tell thee of (Gen. 22:1, 2).

Sometimes it seems as though we are asked to give up the thing that means most to us. We have been taught, "Jehovah gave, and Jehovah hath taken away; blessed be the name of Jehovah" (Job 1:21). This is only man's belief. However, we should obey that which comes as our highest prompting and trust God in spite of what seems to be a great sacrifice on our part. Obedience is a foundation for faith. Abraham believed that whatever God told him to do was for the best, no matter what the appearance was. Until we learn to love righteousness more than personal wishes our faith is not very strong. Have we not struggled with ourselves and finally decided to do what we felt we should, despite its being difficult? Our very willingness to do what we believe to be right will save us from any great hardship. We may have to go to the very brink of disaster, however: Abraham had tied Isaac to the wood altar and had taken his knife in hand to slay his son:

> And the angel of Jehovah called unto him out of heaven, and said, Abraham, Abraham: and he said, Here am I. And he said, Lay not thy hand upon the lad, neither do thou anything unto him; for now I know that thou fearest God, seeing thou hast not withheld thy son, thine only son, from me. And Abraham lifted up his eyes, and looked, and, behold, behind *him* a ram caught in the thicket by his horns: and Abraham went and took the ram, and offered him up for a burnt-offering in the stead of his son (Gen. 22:11-13).

The animal represents strong, unredeemed thoughts of sense, and these the Lord calls upon us to sacrifice. For his obedience Abraham was rewarded by a confirmation of God's promise of greatness.

CHAPTER IV

Jacob

Genesis 27-50

O NE OF THE loveliest stories in the Old Testament is of the romance and marriage of Isaac and Rebekah. Abraham did not want his son Isaac to marry a daughter of the Canaanites, so he sent a servant to Haran, where Terah had settled when he moved from the southern part of Mesopotamia and where members of Abraham's own family still lived. Under divine guidance the servant selected Rebekah, the sister of Laban, for Isaac's wife. Rebekah represents "the soul's natural delight in beauty. . . . The happy Isaac consciousness claims its counterpart in Rebekah" (M.D. 547).

Of this union twin sons were born, Esau and Jacob. From the description of the two brothers and the meaning of their names (Esau means "hairy, rough," and Jacob means "supplanter") (M.D. 206, 313) it is apparent that Esau represents the physical and Jacob the mental phase of consciousness. Man is first aware of himself as a physical being; as he develops, the mental takes precedence over the physical; supplants it. This is a step in the evolution of man's consciousness.

As Esau was born first he was the direct heir of Isaac. Jacob, however, yearned to obtain his brother's birthright. The birthright not only meant property and power in a material sense, but it had another

significance that Jacob perceived. Isaac's legacy to
his elder son was the covenant between the Lord
and Abraham, which had been reaffirmed to Isaac.
The fulfillment of the covenant was a spiritual obligation, and Esau, having no conception of it as
a sacred mission, could not have carried it on. His
interest was wholly in the physical realm. Jacob, on
the other hand, discerned the full value of the birthright.

This tells us that man, when dominated by his
mentality, is closer to the spiritual plane than when
he is ruled by his physical nature. Knowing his
brother's weakness, Jacob played upon it and offered
Esau a mess of pottage when he was hungry, demanding the birthright as a price. Throughout the
ages, men (like Esau) have bartered their spiritual
inheritance for physical satisfaction. They turn aside
from a rightful obligation because it interferes with
their pleasures; they depart from strict honesty to
make a sharp deal in business.

The mentality, which Jacob at this stage represents, is not above reproach. Its vision is greater
and it has increased powers of discernment, but zeal
often obscures righteousness. To Jacob's way of
thinking, the end justified the means. The same
thought lies behind the stolen blessing. Certain types
of mind are given to deceitful practices. When the
time came for Isaac to give his blessing to Esau,
Jacob masqueraded as his brother, and Isaac, thinking that he was bestowing the blessing upon his
favorite son Esau gave it to Jacob instead. It is

inevitable that in the unfoldment of man's consciousness the mind must supplant the physical nature, but there is always a penalty if right motive does not substantiate right action.

When Esau discovered that Jacob had secured Isaac's blessing, which should have been his, he threatened Jacob's life. Rebekah influenced Isaac to agree that Jacob should seek a wife among the daughters of their kinsmen in Mesopotamia. At her instigation Jacob left Canaan. He started toward Haran, where lived Laban, Rebekah's brother. The metaphysical meaning of the name Haran is "an exalted state of mind" (M.D. 256), and Jacob's journey in that direction represents man's reaching out for a clearer spiritual vision. This Jacob received. When he reached Bethel he "tarried there all night, because the sun was set" (Gen. 28:11). During the night he had a vision of a ladder reaching from earth to heaven on which the angels of God ascended and descended, "and, behold, Jehovah stood above it" (Gen. 28:13). The ladder is symbolical of the connection between God and man, the spiritual and the human. Man's cardinal sin is a belief in separation between God and man. But we should not lose sight of the fact that there is always a contact between the divine and the human. The rungs of the ladder signify varying degrees of consciousness between the human plane of thought and the spiritual realm. Angels are man's pure thoughts, which ascend to God in prayer and descend to man laden with inspiration.

Here Jehovah confirmed the covenant to Jacob:

I am Jehovah, the God of Abraham thy father, and the God of Isaac: the land whereon thou liest, to thee will I give it, and to thy seed; and thy seed shall be as the dust of the earth . . . and in thee and in thy seed shall all the families of the earth be blessed. And, behold, I am with thee, and will keep thee withersoever thou goest, and will bring thee again unto this land; for I will not leave thee, until I have done that which I have spoken to thee of (Gen. 28:13-15).

When Jacob awakened he exclaimed:

Surely Jehovah is in this place; and I knew it not. And he was afraid, and said, How dreadful is this place! this is none other than the house of God, and this is the gate of heaven (Gen. 28:16).

This represents man's realization of the divine omnipresence. "Wherever I am, God is." Some perception of this is requisite for our ongoing in Truth. We feel a sense of reverence bordering on awe when we first discern that Jehovah "is in this place." Jacob carried with him thenceforth an awareness of God's presence. Though he was not always true to the vision that came to him at Bethel, he never quite forgot it, and at the time of a supreme test he had the necessary spiritual endurance.

When Jacob reached Haran he entered the employ of his uncle Laban, and fell in love with Laban's youngest daughter Rachel. In those days a payment of money or service was required for a wife, and Jacob agreed to work for Laban seven years in payment for Rachel. "And they seemed unto him but a

few days, for the love he had to her" (Gen. 29:20).
But "God is not mocked: for whatsoever a man
soweth, that shall he also reap" (Gal. 6:7). Jacob
had deceived his father Isaac and cheated his brother
Esau, and the law of compensation operated to bring
back to him what he had given. When the time came
for Jacob's marriage to Rachel, Laban deceived Jacob
and gave him his older daughter Leah. Jacob was
not to be outdone: he worked seven more years for
his beloved Rachel. If, when the law gives us our just
deserts, we can meet an experience constructively,
we shall always go forward.

There was compensation also for the unloved
Leah. She became the mother of six of Jacob's sons,
Reuben, Simeon, Levi, Judah, Issachar, and Zebulun;
also she had a daughter, Dinah. After Levi was born,
Rachel was so distressed that she had no child that
she gave Jacob Bilhah, her maid, of whom two sons
were born, Dan and Naphtali. This made Leah
jealous and she gave Jacob her maid Zilpah who
also bore him two sons, Gad and Asher. Finally
Rachel's prayer for children was answered, and she
had two sons, Joseph and Benjamin. The twelve sons
of Jacob became the founders of the twelve tribes of
Israel. Metaphysically they represent the twelve
spiritual faculties of man, as do the Twelve Apostles.

Eventually Jacob decided to leave Laban and return to Canaan. Laban knew that his wealth had
been greatly increased through Jacob and he did
not want his son-in-law to leave. However, upon
Jacob's insistence, Laban agreed to divide the flocks

and herds according to Jacob's suggestion, which was that he, Jacob, take the speckled and the spotted and the black animals from among the herds. Laban thought to get the better of Jacob by removing the speckled and spotted animals, leaving only the plain-colored whose young he would receive. Jacob out-witted him by devising a way to increase the number of speckled and spotted animals.

And Jacob took him rods of fresh poplar, and of the almond and of the plane-tree; and peeled white streaks in them, and made the white appear which was in the rods. And he set the rods which he had peeled over against the flocks in the gutters in the watering-troughs where the flocks came to drink . . . And the flocks conceived before the rods, and the flocks brought forth ringstreaked, speckled, and spotted (Gen. 30:37-39).

This emphasizes the fundamental truth of life that we reproduce that to which we give attention. Whatever we look at (perceive) we bring forth, whether it be good or ill. When we learn to have the "single" eye toward the spiritual, we become Godlike. Paul confirms this by saying, "We all, with unveiled face beholding as in a mirror the glory of the Lord, are transformed into the same image from glory to glory, even as from the Lord the Spirit" (II Cor. 3:18).

Finally Jacob, his wives, sons, servants, and herds started on their way toward Canaan. Had not Je-hovah said to him at Bethel that He would bring him "again into this land" (Gen. 28:15)? This was the country to which the Lord had guided Abraham.

Though it was best for Jacob to be in Babylonia for a time, it was inevitable that he would return to the good (land) promised by the Lord. Even so, man eventually returns to the place that God designates for his good.

On the way to Canaan Jacob received word that Esau was coming toward him with an armed force. Jacob immediately thought that his brother was seeking revenge. Would Esau try to kill Jacob and take his possessions? Jacob still had a guilty conscience regarding Esau and he was very much afraid. He did the two things anyone should do when confronted with a trial: first, he prayed; second, he acted wisely in an outer way. In this case the logical outer action was to send gifts to his brother to convince Esau of his desire to make amends. Then, sending his entire company ahead, Jacob remained alone at the ford of the Jabbok. "And there wrestled a man with him until the breaking of the day" (Gen. 32:24).

The "man" with whom Jacob struggled was his higher self. This is symbolic of the conflict between the human and the divine that takes place in each of us. Even Jesus had to meet the Tempter in the wilderness, but He rose instantly above each temptation. With Jacob it was a struggle, for he had not yet come into full possession of spiritual powers. His thigh was thrown out of joint but he did not give up. In this case the thigh represents the personal self, which often must suffer a hurt. If we contend with our higher nature, there come times when personal pride is injured, self-esteem wounded, strength exhausted. But we should hold fast to the spiritual even as Jacob did, and cry, "I will not let thee go, except thou bless me" (Gen. 32:26). God always has a blessing for us in every experience, no matter how trying, and we must not let go of Him until we receive it. Sometimes it seems as if the Lord is bent on deserting us; then our challenge is to hold on until the breaking of the day.

And he [the man] said unto him [Jacob], What is thy name? And he said, Jacob. And he said, Thy name shall be called no more Jacob, but Israel: for thou hast striven with God and with men, and hast prevailed. . . . And he blessed him there (Gen. 32:27-29).

The name Israel means "striving for God" and also "a prince with God" (M.D. 303). In the early stages of spiritual growth we "strive for God" but when we meet and overcome the lower impulses we become like the one who was called "a prince with God." "Israel is the real of man, that consciousness which is founded in God" (M.D. 304). The experience of Jacob at the ford Jabbok represents the ascendance of the spiritual over the human. Before this occurrence Jacob had been afraid of his brother; after it, he went to meet Esau at the head of his company. Nothing is fearsome when we meet it as a prince of God. The brothers were reconciled.

Even though we make great spiritual progress we still have to meet trials, the seeds of which were sown in less enlightened days. Jacob's daughter Dinah was defiled by Shechem, a prince of one of the tribes of Canaan, and in avenging this two of her brothers, Simeon and Levi, so antagonized Shechem's tribe that Jacob and his family left that portion of the land in fear. They went to Bethel. There, as on the former occasion when Jacob had the vision of the ladder, the Lord was revealed to him. "And Jacob set up a pillar in the place where he spake with him, a pillar of stone: and he poured out a drink-offering thereon, and poured oil thereon" (Gen. 35:14).

In time of trouble we need spiritual consolation, which always comes through prayer, and the experience is commemorated in our own consciousness. Divine guidance was given, and Jacob journeyed to Ephrath (Bethlehem). On the way Benjamin was born, and Rachel died. At Mamre Isaac passed to the beyond, and Jacob was left to carry on the birthright and blessing that Isaac had bequeathed him.

With the 37th chapter of Genesis the story of Joseph begins. "Joseph represents the 'increasing' faculty of the mind, that state of consciousness in which we increase in all phases of our character. This is especially true of substance; for Joseph, as imagination, molds mind substance in the realm of forms" (Mys. of Gen. 293).

Jacob gave to his son Joseph a coat of many colors, which has an interesting spiritual significance.

The coat is the symbol of the Truth given to us by the Father. Truth in its entirety is symbolized by the seamless garment worn by Jesus, for it cannot be separated into divisions or parts. All truth is one Truth. Joseph's coat's being of many colors indicates that when we open up this new realm of consciousness and begin to use the imagination, our conception of Truth is colored by the many previous mental states that have so long herded our flocks of thoughts. At this stage we have not yet come into the understanding, into the pure white light of unqualified Truth, that is symbolized by the seamless robe of unity (Mys. of Gen. 294, 295).

Joseph was the favorite son of Jacob, as he was the first child of the beloved wife Rachel. This aroused the jealousy of his ten half brothers, and Joseph increased their animosity by telling them of a dream that implied their subservience to him. Before the faculty of imagination (which Joseph represents) (M.D. 366) is spiritualized it may have delusions of grandeur regarding personality, and this is always a forerunner of disaster. Undoubtedly Joseph aided in bringing hardship upon himself, but he met and conquered it courageously. He learned to work in harmony with the Lord, to do His will, to speak His word. Each misfortune—being sold by his brothers into slavery, the unjust accusation in the house of Potiphar, being cast into prison and rendering service for which, at the time, he was not rewarded—was but a steppingstone to greater heights.

We are told "Jehovah was with Joseph" (Gen. 39:21). The Lord is always with everyone, but only he who realizes it is able to rise above adversity. Finally Joseph's great opportunity came. He was summoned to interpret Pharaoh's dream, and he showed wisdom and humility: "It is not in me: God will give Pharaoh an answer of peace" (Gen. 41:16).

Pharaoh's dream meant that there would be seven plenteous years followed by seven years of famine. The Egyptian ruler was so impressed by the interpretation that he put Joseph in charge of the land. "Only in the throne will I be greater than thou," he promised (Gen. 41:40).

During the years of famine Joseph's ten brothers came from Canaan to buy grain in Egypt. We might wonder why Joseph did not make himself known to them immediately and forgive them. Perhaps the answer lies in the fact that a person cannot receive forgiveness until he has risen above the state of consciousness that he was in when he committed an unjust act. At the time Joseph was sold into slavery his brothers hated him and were willing to sacrifice him to their advantage; neither were they mindful of their father Jacob's sorrow. However, when they came to Egypt the second time and Joseph, unrecognized by them, demanded that Benjamin be left in Egypt, the brothers volunteered to sacrifice themselves for his brother. Judah was the spokesman for the group, and his plea that Benjamin be allowed to return to Jacob and Judah himself remain a prisoner is indeed a moving one. The brothers were worthy of forgiveness, and Joseph gave it outwardly as he had long before given it inwardly. Joseph realized that the experience was not without divine intent and said to his brothers, "Now be not grieved, nor angry with yourselves, that ye sold me hither: for God did send me before you to preserve life" (Gen. 45:5).

On another occasion he said, "Ye meant evil

against me; but God meant it for good" (Gen. 50:
20). No matter how much of seeming evil comes
into our lives, if we remember that God's will for us
is always good we shall be able to turn the trial into
a blessing.

Joseph settled his father and brothers in the
section of Egypt known as Goshen, and there they
prospered. Jacob's last days were spent in peace and
happiness. He blessed his sons and the two sons of
Joseph, Ephraim and Manasseh, thus giving Joseph
an additional inheritance among the tribes of Israel.

And Joseph lived a hundred and ten years. . . . And
Joseph said unto his brethren, I die; but God will surely
visit you, and bring you up out of this land unto the land
which he sware to Abraham, to Isaac, and to Jacob. . . .
and ye shall carry up my bones from hence (Gen. 50:22,
24-25).

Joseph, a type of the Christ, performs a service in
Egypt, the lower realm of consciousness, yet knows
that Egypt is not the permanent home of the spiritual. His prediction that the family of Jacob would
return to Canaan and his request that his bones
be carried hence indicate his understanding that
man should return to his source, Spirit. It is interesting to note that four centuries later his wish
was granted literally, for when the Israelites left
Egypt under the leadership of Moses they took with
them the bones of Joseph. The bones were finally
buried by Joshua in Shechem, where Jacob had lived
for a time.

CHAPTER V

Moses

Part I—Exodus 1-19

I N OUR SPIRITUAL progress we may pass through many experiences from the time faith is first quickened in us until we come into a comprehension of the law of the Lord, which governs the universe and man. The lives of Abraham, Isaac, and Jacob are typical of some of the experiences through which we pass ere we stand on the firm ground of the understanding of divine law.

The law was not revealed to Abraham. His sustaining power was faith, but before faith can come into full growth it must have as its foundation an understanding of God as law. The Scripture says of Abraham, "And he believed in Jehovah; and he reckoned it to him for righteousness" (Gen. 15:6). However, Jesus said that every jot or tittle of the law must be fulfilled and He declared that His purpose was not to destroy the law but to fulfill it.

We perceive that during the Patriarchal period man was going forward steadily in his spiritual development. There were lapses, to be sure, but the trend was definitely upward. Then a slump came, depicted by the enslavement of the Hebrews in Egypt. Faith without understanding is insufficient; such faith gradually deteriorates to the sense level, becoming the servant of worldly pride, power, and greed (Egypt). However, the one who has once begun his journey to spiritual freedom is not permitted to retrogress indefinitely. Moses, who represents metaphysically an understanding of God as law, comes forth and does his mighty work.

Moses' life is divided into three periods of approximately forty years each. The first of these was spent in Egypt, where he was born of a Hebrew couple of the tribe of Levi, Amram and Jochebed. At that time the Hebrews had been in the land of the Nile some four centuries, living in the northeastern section of the area called Goshen. There they prospered and multiplied exceedingly. Eventually "there arose a new king over Egypt, who knew not Joseph" (Exod. 1:8) and made slaves of the Hebrews. Their lot became a bitter one. Because of their great numbers, Pharaoh decreed that all male children of the Hebrews be killed at birth. The story of how Moses' mother hid her infant son in the bulrushes and how the child was discovered by Pharaoh's daughter is a familiar one.

Moses grew to manhood at the royal court of Egypt, where he had the advantage of the best education the age afforded. This marked the period of his intellectual development. A trained mind is necessary for one who is to become a good leader of his people. Moses knew that he was a Hebrew and rebelled at the cruel treatment inflicted upon his race. One day he saw an Egyptian beating a Hebrew and, in anger, he killed the Egyptian. For this he was forced to flee Egypt to save his life, and he went to Midian, a desert lying between Egypt and Canaan.

With this change he entered upon the second period of forty years. In Midian he became a shepherd for Jethro, a priest, and married Jethro's daughter Zipporah. It might seem as if Moses, by his rash act of slaying the Egyptian, had forfeited his opportunity to be of service to his enslaved kinsmen. He had made the grave mistake of attempting to force justice. He did not yet know how great are the things that are accomplished "not by might, nor by power, but by my Spirit, saith Jehovah of hosts" (Zech. 4:6).

Being compelled to leave Egypt was the penalty Moses paid for the sin he committed. But no matter what hardship we undergo as a result of our transgression, if we meet it courageously and with faith we learn the very lesson we need most. Before Moses could become a great leader he had to gain spiritual enlightenment, and this he gained during his sojourn to Midian. The life of a shepherd was lonely, providing ample opportunity for thought, meditation, and prayer. Humanly speaking, it must have been a trial for the capable Moses, but that he met it spiritually is attested by the author of The Epistle to the Hebrews who wrote of this period of Moses' life, "he endured, as seeing him who is invisible" (Heb. 11:27). The great invisible presence is God, and whenever we keep our attention on Him while undergoing a difficult experience, in the right way and at the right time our release will come.

"Now Moses was keeping the flock of Jethro . . . and he led the flock to the back of the wilderness,

and came to the mountain of God, unto Horeb"
(Exod. 3:1).

Undoubtedly Moses had often led his flock there.
Horeb means "solitude" (M.D. 284) and, metaphysically, it represents a high spiritual realization
or the silence. Do we not lead our flock (thoughts
and emotions) to the quietness of the inner realm?
We cannot know at what hour the Lord will come.
Sometimes we seem to watch for Him in vain, but
if we are faithful in prayer we shall eventually feel
His presence and hear His word.

And the angel of Jehovah appeared unto him in a
flame of fire out of the midst of a bush; and he looked,
and, behold, the bush burned with fire, and the bush was
not consumed. And Moses said, I will turn aside now, and
see this great sight, why the bush is not burnt. And when
Jehovah saw that he turned aside to see, God called unto
him out of the midst of the bush, and said, Moses, Moses.
And he said, Here am I (Exod. 3:2-4).

This was an experience in cosmic consciousness,
a full realization of the divine presence. God calls
us again and again, but we have to be in a high
state of consciousness to hear Him and respond.

And he said, Draw not nigh hither: put off thy shoes
from off thy feet, for the place whereon thou standest is
holy ground (Exod. 3:5).

We are always standing in the presence of the
Lord. Do we know it and show reverence for it,
(take off our shoes)? We seem to stand on very
ordinary earth, though in reality it is holy.

A beautiful prayer by Charles Fillmore begins,

"I am now in the presence of pure Being, and immersed in the Holy Spirit of life, love, and wisdom." We live, move, and have our being in the divine life, and when we are aware of it we look and listen in reverent humility.

Three great truths were revealed to Moses:

1. God wishes all people to be free. "I have surely seen the affliction of my people that are in Egypt, and have heard their cry . . . and I am come down to deliver them out of the hand of the Egyptians" (Exod. 3:7, 8).

Metaphysically man may be said to be in Egypt when he is suffering any sort of limitation, sickness, poverty, unhappiness. It is God's will that he be free. "I will; be thou made clean" (Matt. 8:3).

2. God has prepared a place for all His children. "I am come . . . to bring them up out of that land unto a good land and a large, unto a land flowing with milk and honey" (Exod. 3:8).

Man does not create his own good. It has already been prepared for him by his Lord. The Promised Land is now for every man, established by the Almighty since the foundation of the world. Health, plenty, peace, and joy exist in the invisible realm and form the necessary ingredients for all outer good.

3. Understanding of God as law (Moses) must lead man from bondage to liberty (Egypt to Canaan). "Come now therefore, and I will send thee unto Pharaoh, that thou mayest bring forth my people the children of Israel out of Egypt" (Exod. 3: 10).

The Moses faculty in man must guide the unredeemed but aspiring elements of his own consciousness (Children of Israel) from the darkness of sense thought to the light of an increased spiritual realization. From this spiritual height man views the Promised Land, or the good that God has prepared for him.

While Moses was grateful that God willed freedom for his people, he doubted his own ability to rescue them from Egypt. Various obstacles came to his mind: he feared that the Israelites would not believe that Jehovah had commissioned him; he was slow of speech and felt that he would not be able to convince them of his divine mission. Moses argued, also, that Pharaoh would not allow the Hebrew slaves to leave his land and he, Moses, was without power to compel the mighty ruler. Moses' objections arose from the human way of viewing matters, as is often the case with us. In prayer we are inspired as to what to do, but are sometimes afraid to try. We do not believe we have the power, nor do we think we can get the necessary co-operation from others. We should remember that when there is the spiritual prompting to act there is also the spiritual power to do so. The Lord told Moses to say to the Children of Israel:

I AM hath sent me unto you. . . . Jehovah, the God of your fathers, the God of Abraham, the God of Isaac, and the God of Jacob, hath sent me unto you: this is my name for ever, and this is my memorial unto all generations (Exod. 3:14, 15).

Charles Fillmore states that Jehovah of the Old Testament and Christ of the New Testament refer to the spiritual self of man, the Spirit of truth, or the I AM, which dwells in him. Therefore, the instruction to Moses was to function from his inner, powerful, spiritual self. "I AM hath sent me unto you." Whenever man goes forth in this spirit, others have confidence in him and will follow him.

Moses' timidity, due to his lack of eloquence, was overcome by having his brother Aaron accompany him as spokesman. Also the Lord said to Moses, "Now therefore go and I will be with thy mouth, and teach thee what thou shalt speak" (Exod. 4:12). Moses was likewise instructed how to use his rod. It was an ordinary shepherd's crook, but when Moses cast it down it brought disaster and when he raised it, it brought a blessing. Mr. Fillmore states, "the rod represents spiritual power" (M.D. Add. II). When used rightly it is the means of bringing miracles to pass.

Moses set out on his mission promptly. He did not let his inspiration fade in the false light of mortal reasoning. He and Aaron won the confidence of the Israelites, but Pharaoh refused to release his Hebrew servants. Pharaoh represents the sense consciousness, which is attached to material things (M.D. 519). Moses called down nine plagues upon the Egyptians, and after each one Pharaoh agreed to permit the Children of Israel to leave. However as each plague was removed, Pharaoh rescinded his permission.

We are told that "Jehovah hardened the heart of Pharaoh" (Exod. 9:12). This is one of those cryptic statements in the Bible that seem to imply inconsistency on the part of a good God. The explanation lies in the fact that we often pervert God's just law through the wrong use of it and establish destructive attitudes of consciousness that act as a law or governing power in our lives. For example, a person who gives way to anger repeatedly builds up a habit of unrighteous action for himself, and though he may attempt to overcome it, he finds himself caught in its meshes again and again. Pharaoh had permitted selfishness and greed to rule him. When the plagues came his fear of them was stronger than his habitual state of mind, and, in order to be freed of a plague, he granted Moses' request that the Children of Israel be released. But when the plague was lifted, his habit of selfishness reasserted itself. The law that he let rule his being had become his lord and master, and it "hardened" his heart.

Moses benefited from Pharaoh's continued refusal, though he would hardly have recognized the repeated refusals as a benefit. They taught him perseverance. Often our answer to prayer does not come after our first prayer. We do not overcome Pharaoh (sense consciousness) with one trial. Repeated efforts are necessary, and unless we are willing to try again and again, we cannot free our Children of Israel from Egypt.

The tenth and last plague was the slaying of the first-born of the Egyptians and the first-born of their cattle. The Israelites were not affected. Those who trust God are protected from disaster. Moses instructed each Hebrew family to sacrifice a lamb and sprinkle its blood on the door of their house. Jehovah would then "pass over" (Exod. 12:13) the home and it would not be visited by the plague. This is the origin of what came to be known as the Passover, a sacred day for the Jews even until this time. It also has a profound metaphysical significance relating to the regeneration of the body through the purifying of the consciousness. Of this the *Metaphysical Bible Dictionary* says (page 504):

The whole man must be pure, and his inner life must be made so open and free that he will not be afraid to blazon it upon the very doors of his house where all who pass may read. Then the Lord will execute His judgment, and those who have purified the life of the lamb (or the body) will escape the messenger (or thought) of death.

This final plague wrought such distress in Egypt that Pharaoh was forced to consent to the departure of the Children of Israel. They left, rejoicing. However, when they reached the Red Sea they discovered that Pharaoh and his hosts were pursuing them. It seemed as if they were between Scylla and Charybdis. They wept and reviled Moses, accusing him of leading them there to die.

And Moses said unto the people, Fear ye not, stand still, and see the salvation of Jehovah, which he will work for you to-day . . . Jehovah will fight for you, and ye shall hold your peace (Exod. 14:13, 14).

Then Moses lifted up his rod and stretched forth his hand over the sea. The waters divided, and the Children of Israel went through on dry land. When the Egyptians attempted to follow, the waters of the sea returned and the host of Egypt perished.

There comes a time when man makes his escape from the realm of the sense consciousness (represented by Egypt), but he is still far from being on a permanently spiritual level of activity. As Truth students we have left Egypt but have not reached the Promised Land. There is an interim period, typified in the Old Testament by the wilderness, in which we may wander for a long time as did the Children of Israel. This period of approximately forty years was the third period of Moses' life and the most important one.

The experiences of the Israelites in the wilderness are typical of the ups and downs through which we pass in our spiritual ongoing. These people desired to do the will of the Lord. Had they not left Egypt under Moses' guidance? But when calamities arose they lost heart and lamented their lot. On one occasion they had no water and when they discovered an oasis they found to their consternation that the water there was too bitter to drink.

And the people murmured against Moses, saying, What shall we drink? And he cried unto Jehovah; and Jehovah showed him a tree, and he cast it into the waters, and the waters were made sweet (Exod. 15:24, 25).

We must learn to sweeten bitter experiences

(waters). Only the Lord can tell us how and, like
Moses, we should cry to Him. He will show us
what element to use—and it is always something
close at hand.

Then they had no food. Again Moses prayed,
and manna fell. There is always the divine provision
for us, and we receive it if we pray. Our need is
summed up in Jesus' prayer, "Give us this day our
daily bread" (Matt. 6:11). The manna was literally
and figuratively the daily bread of the Israelites.
It was physical food to sustain them, but it also represented all that was required for the day: faith,
courage, and intelligence. When man functions in
the human consciousness he is never content with
enough for the present. He wants to be sure there
will be plenty for years to come, because he lacks
a sense of security. When he feeds on spiritual
manna, the divine qualities God has given him, he
is content with what is sufficient for his outer needs
and has faith that it will be provided day by day.
The manna could not be hoarded because it spoiled,
but there was always enough to satisfy the daily
hunger. When we come to the realization that God
is the great provider and thank Him for His food,
both physical and spiritual, we have some conception
of the full meaning of the manna that nourished
the Israelites throughout their sojourn in the wilderness.

Again, the Children of Israel were thirsty. This
time the Lord told Moses to smite the rock, and
when he did water gushed forth. Enemies attacked

them, but as long as Moses held up his hand with the rod of God in it the Israelites were victorious. When Moses grew weary and dropped his hand, the enemy (Amalek) prevailed. So Aaron and Hur held up Moses' hands. Sometimes we grow weary with holding up our hand (keeping the consciousness on a spiritual level). Then it is that we should ask others who know the Truth to sustain us, even as Hur and Aaron held up the hands of Moses.

Finally, the Hebrew company reached the mount called Sinai or Horeb. This marked the first long rest in their journey, and it was there that Moses received a revelation of the law of God. Having gained an understanding of the divine presence (revelation at the burning bush), Moses had to receive definite instructions for spiritual ideals and action. If we consider the law as given to him merely as a great code of ethics belonging to an age far-gone, we lose its real significance, even though we may know our own modern ethical code is based on it. The law is not only a statement of God's will but it gives instructions for righteous living. As it was finally developed by the Jews long after the time of Moses, the law was in three parts: (1) the Commandments (Decalogue), (2) the Judgments, governing the social life of Israel, (3) the Ordinances, governing the religious life of Israel. Most important, as far as we are concerned, is the first part, the Ten Commandments. A spiritual interpretation of the Decalogue will be given in the following chapter.

CHAPTER VI

Moses

Part II—Exodus; Numbers; Deuteronomy

THE DECALOGUE in the Old Testament and the Sermon on the Mount in the New Testament are the greatest annunciations of righteous thinking and living yet given to mankind. The first bears the same relation to Judaism that the second does to Christianity, and from Moses and Jesus, the founders of these two great religions, came words that spell the redemption of humanity.

Some cynics maintain that the human race is as far from understanding and obeying them today as it was when the voice of Moses thundered from Mount Sinai. Certainly men have not used them fully as a pattern for conduct, yet the advance in civilization since Moses' time can, to a large degree, be measured by mankind's assimilation and practice of these two great teachings. Many of their precepts are included in all the living religions of the world.

Since the beginning of recorded history men have longed and fought for freedom but only occasionally have a few perceived that the boon they so ardently sought is not of the body but of the mind. "Ye shall know the truth, and the truth shall make you free" (John 8:32). In the Decalogue and in the Sermon on the Mount is Truth found in all its pristine splendor. It is beautiful, majestic, inspiring. It is ours to comprehend and to absorb with mind and heart.

"And Jehovah came down upon mount Sinai, to the top of the mount: and Jehovah called Moses . . . and Moses went up" (Exod. 19:20).

Man receives inspiration only when he ascends the mount or high place in consciousness.

"And God spake all these words, saying, I am Jehovah thy God, who brought thee out of the land of Egypt, out of the house of bondage" (Exod. 20:1, 2).

Exodus 20:3-17 contains the Ten Commandments. They have an outer or literal meaning, and also an inner or spiritual meaning. We are particularly concerned with their spiritual interpretation.

1. Thou shalt have no other gods before me.

We are not to recognize any life, presence, or power save God. He is the supreme ruler of the cosmos; He is the source, the origin of all there is. "There is but one presence and one power in the universe, God the good, omnipotent," is a familiar statement in our Unity teaching. However, we are prone to believe and acknowledge another power, the Devil or evil. Whatever we recognize as the ruling authority of our lives is our god.

2. Thou shalt not make unto thee a graven image.

Although men may no longer make stone or metal images of gods to worship as did the ancient peoples, they do make gods of things and personalities. Money, fame, and pleasure are popular gods of the present. Some bow down and worship persons to whom they entrust their happiness and look for support and protection. There is but one God, invisible, all-powerful, and everlasting. He has no corporeal form but is everywhere evenly present as life and substance. So long as we try to confine Him to time, space, or form, we are making a "graven image" and thus breaking the second commandment.

3. *Thou shalt not take the name of Jehovah thy God in vain.*

Surely we would not use the name of God in a profane sense. Yet we often take His name in vain by connecting it with some negative condition, such as we are doing when we say, "I am sick," or "I am poor." I AM is God's name in us. Let us be sure to associate it with a quality that belongs to His nature. Affirmations of Truth help to train us in the right use of God's name. Jesus said, "I am the light of the world" (John 8:12). "I am the good shepherd" (John 10:11). He constantly identified Himself with the reality of Being.

4. *Remember the sabbath day, to keep it holy.*

In their efforts to keep this commandment, the Jews of ancient times formulated strict rules to make man for the Sabbath instead of realizing that "the sabbath was made for man" (Mark 2:27) as Jesus said. Spiritually, the command has to do with the sort of inner Sabbath we keep. The word Sabbath means rest (M.D. 562). When we rest in the Lord, which we do in all true prayer, the consciousness is holy and is uncontaminated by mundane thoughts.

We find that the first four commandments govern our right relationship to God, and the last six govern our right relationship to our fellow men.

5. *Honor thy father and thy mother.*

Outwardly this is an admonition to esteem our earthly parents. Not only are they responsible for our physical being but their devotion and care provided the necessities for existence in our early life. Right adjustment in the realm of human relationships begins with proper respect for the first persons we knew, our parents. The spiritual fulfillment of this commandment lies in our reverence for our Creator, in whom the father quality of wisdom is joined with the mother quality of love. The masculine and feminine attributes are likewise present in each of us, for "in the image of God created he him; male and female created he them" (Gen. 1:27). When we honor the source from which we came, our Father-Mother (God), we draw understanding and love therefrom, both of which are requisites of true worship and result in a balanced development of our spiritual nature.

6. *Thou shalt not kill.*

Man has no right to deprive anyone of life, for he cannot give life. To obey this commandment spiritually, we should be careful not to destroy another's courage or faith. Everyone has a right to "life, liberty, and the pursuit of happiness," and when man, in personal will and power, deprives his brothers of these, he may be said to "kill" them.

7. *Thou shalt not commit adultery.*

This is the commandment that has to do with moral, clean living. No one should entertain the

hope of complete spiritual expression who has not
learned to comply with the highest code, both in his
personal life and in his dealings with others. Spiritually, to "commit adultery" is to adulterate or
weaken the higher consciousness by the injection of
carnal thoughts and emotions.

8. Thou shalt not steal.

Outwardly, this refers to another aspect of the
moral law. Man should not take that which is not
his. Thieves are considered outside the pale of de-
cent society, yet there is a thievery that is just as
wrong in God's sight as breaking into a man's house
and taking his possessions. Spiritually, the significance of this commandment lies deeper: dictators
rob men of freedom, strong-minded persons rob
others of free will; many a doting mother robs her
children of their right to make decisions and to live
their own lives as they choose.

*9. Thou shalt not bear false witness against
thy neighbor.*

Literally, this commandment cautions us not to
tell an untruth about anyone. Much of gossip is a
violation of this commandment. Considered in a spiritual sense, we are bearing false witness against another when we speak of him in a human, limited
way. We should behold people as they are in Truth,
sons of the Most High. When we connect them with
all sorts of negative conditions we are bearing "false
witness." Criticism, condemnation, and judging by
the appearance are ways of violating the ninth commandment.

10. Thou shalt not covet.

Covetousness is a moral as well as a spiritual sin. This commandment is disobeyed as often as the first commandment, and as unthinkingly. Wars are fought because one nation covets what another has; families are broken up because someone desires the husband or wife. Avarice, envy, jealousy, and selfishness are closely allied to covetousness. As we grow in spiritual stature, we realize that we never need the good another has. All good is from God, whose presence is constantly with us. Nothing can deprive us of it except our own inability to receive.

Obedience to the Ten Commandments stands, and always will, as the foundation stone upon which our spiritual structure is built. The commandments should be obeyed in the letter and in the spirit. An attempt to conform to the letter alone makes for self-righteousness. It is impossible, however, to obey them in their highest spiritual sense without obeying them literally also.

It was on the mount also that Moses received instructions for the building of the Tabernacle. The Tabernacle, like the temple and church of today, is symbolic of God's presence among men. However, the true tabernacle is not the building but the spirit of worship. Moses was told to build according to the pattern shown him in the mount. That is the way we build our tabernacle also, in compliance with the inspiration received when we are in a prayerful and spiritual state of consciousness.

At Jehovah's direction Moses selected Aaron his

brother to be the high priest. The name Aaron means "illumined" (M.D. 9), and metaphysically Aaron represents the "executive power of divine law." Aaron belonged to the tribe of Levi, which henceforth became the priestly tribe. The sons of Aaron inherited the position of high priest, while other members of the tribe served in the Tabernacle and later in the Temple.

When the Children of Israel had completed the Tabernacle,

Then the cloud covered the tent of meeting, and the glory of Jehovah filled the tabernacle. . . . And when the cloud was taken up from over the tabernacle, the children of Israel went onward, throughout all their journeys; but if the cloud was not taken up, then they journeyed not till the day that it was taken up. For the cloud of Jehovah was upon the tabernacle by day, and there was fire therein by night, in the sight of all the house of Israel, throughout all their journeys (Exod. 40:34-38).

The cloud by day and the pillar of fire by night are symbols of divine guidance. When we build the Tabernacle (spiritual state of consciousness) and are faithful in worship, the light of the Lord will ever direct our ways.

Finally, the Children of Israel came to Kadesh-barnea, an oasis in the wilderness of Paran. Far in the distance, yet visible to sight, was the southern border of the land of Canaan. Moses selected a man from each tribe and sent the twelve to search out the land. They returned with the report that the country was rich indeed but that it was inhabited by warlike tribes. Ten of the spies counseled against attempting to take it. Only two, Caleb, of the tribe of Judah, and Joshua, of the tribe of Ephraim, said, "Let us go up at once, and possess it; for we are well able to overcome it" (Num. 13:30). The majority ruled against these two, and as a result of the Israelites' lack of faith in the Lord, who had promised them the land, the divine decree was that only Caleb and Joshua of the entire adult company would enter Canaan.

Have not we, too, stood at some Kadesh-barnea from which we could discern the blessings God has for us and yet been afraid to claim them? Why do we not go forward and possess the land? "We are well able to overcome it." Our fear in the power of destructive forces is often greater than our faith in God's promises. Foes, such as sickness, poverty, and inharmony, seem formidable. They are veritable "sons of Anak" (Num. 13:33), tall as giants, and we seem in our own sight as "grasshoppers" compared to them.

The Lord is with us in the acquisition of any good. When we are aware of this and yet afraid to take what is rightfully ours, there is a penalty to be paid. We retrogress temporarily, that is, so far as our spiritual unfoldment is concerned, and may even lose some of the blessings we have heretofore gained. For forty years the Israelites wandered in the wilderness, attacked by savage tribes, disappointed and often rebellious. During that time a new generation grew up. Does this not tell us that we must have a new generation of thoughts, a new consciousness, before we can go forward?

Finally the time of release came, and with a hearty new generation of Hebrews Moses left Kadesh-barnea and went to Mount Hor. There Aaron died, and Eleazar his son became priest. Eleazar means "God is helper" (M.D. 188) and represents "spiritual strength through the recognition of God as his supporting, sustaining power."

And they journeyed from mount Hor by the way to the Red sea, to compass the land of Edom: and the soul of the people was much discouraged because of the way (Num. 21:4).

Someone has said, "When you are discouraged with the outlook, try the uplook." This is what the Children of Israel did. Inspired by Moses, they came to believe that the land of Canaan was their inheritance from the Lord and to put that belief into operation by a determined march in the direction thereof. By defeating the Amorites and the Midianites they acquired the rich country of Gilead. Even Balaam, a prophet who had been hired by Balak, king of Moab, to curse the Israelites and thus attempt to frighten them away, obeyed the Lord and blessed them instead.

Not far from the east bank of the Jordan River they again saw the Land of Promise, but Moses, their great leader, was not to enter it with them.

And Jehovah said unto Moses, Get thee up into this mountain of Abarim, and behold the land which I have given unto the children of Israel. And when thou hast seen it, thou also shalt be gathered unto thy people, as Aaron thy brother was gathered (Num. 27:12-13).

Only Joshua and Caleb of the original adult company were to go into Canaan. Perhaps we have wondered why it was that Moses, who had served his people so valiantly, was not to cross the Jordan with them. The Book of Numbers records that it was because of Moses' and Aaron's disobedience on one occasion during the wilderness wanderings. The Israelites were in need of water, and Moses and Aaron prayed, "and the glory of Jehovah appeared unto them" (Num. 20:6). Moses was instructed, "Speak ye unto the rock . . . that it give forth its water" (Num. 20:8).

Moses and Aaron gathered the assembly together before the rock, and he said unto them, Hear now, ye rebels; shall we bring you forth water out of this rock? And Moses lifted up his hand, and smote the rock with his rod twice; and water came forth abundantly . . . And Jehovah said unto Moses and Aaron, Because ye believed not in me, to sanctify me in the eyes of the children of Israel, therefore ye shall not bring this assembly into the land which I have given them (Num. 20:10-12).

Moses' first sin was anger: "Hear now, ye rebels." The second sin was in taking credit to himself and Aaron: "Shall we bring you forth water?" The third sin lay in striking the rock twice when he had been told to speak to it. However, the punishment seems greater than the sin to our human way of reasoning, and we must seek deeper for the real

secret of Moses' seeming deficiency. Considering the
incident in the light of its spiritual meaning, we
should recall that Moses does not represent the full
spiritual consciousness; he stands for the recognition
and acknowledgment of God as principle or law.
Something must be added, for "love . . . is the ful-
filment of the law" (Rom. 13:10). The author of
The Epistle to the Hebrews writes,

> A previous command is set aside on account of its
> weakness and uselessness (for the Law made nothing
> perfect), and there is introduced a better Hope, by means
> of which we can draw near to God (Heb. 7-18, Moffatt
> translation).

The "better Hope" is the teaching of Jesus that
emphasizes a closer relationship to God through
love. The state of consciousness in which we recognize that there is a divine law and that it should be
obeyed is not sufficient in and of itself. "The Law
made nothing perfect." It does, however, occupy a
very important place in man's unfoldment, for without an understanding of God as law there is no
chance of generating the love to fulfill it. The Moses
consciousness completed its mission by revealing the
Promised Land: the Promised Land must be entered
under the leadership of Joshua, a type of Christ. We
should not think of Moses, the man, as having
failed. He succeeded gloriously in the task set before
him. The truth is, however, that no single spiritual
quality alone is sufficient. Law and love must go
hand in hand; wisdom and will must be balanced, yet
neither is less because it should be united with the

other. The Moses and Joshua qualities combined free us from Egypt (sense consciousness) (Mys. of Gen. 124) and lead us into the Promised Land (the purely spiritual consciousness) (Mys. of Gen. 123).

One of the most inspiring and touching scenes in the Old Testament occurs in the incident in which Moses saw Canaan and realized that he was not to enter it. Instead of having a keen sense of injustice or wailing over his ill-fortune,

Moses spake unto Jehovah, saying, Let Jehovah, the God of the spirits of all flesh, appoint a man over the congregation, who may go out before them, and who may come in before them, and who may lead them out, and who may bring them in; that the congregation of Jehovah be not as sheep which have no shepherd (Num. 27:15-17).

Moses was not thinking of himself but of his people. Such unselfish prayers are always answered:

And Jehovah said unto Moses, Take thee Joshua the son of Nun, a man in whom is the Spirit, and lay thy hand upon him; and set him before Eleazar the priest, and before all the congregation; and give him a charge in their sight. And thou shalt put of thine honor upon him, that all the congregation of the children of Israel may obey. . . . And Moses did as Jehovah commanded him (Num. 27:18-22).

Surely Moses resigned his leadership with the calm of
"One who wraps the drapery of his couch about him,
 And lies down to pleasant dreams."
Humanly considered, he was Israel's creator as a

nation; spiritually considered, he was one of the few
to find "the city which hath the foundations, whose
builder and maker is God" (Heb. 11:10).

So Moses the servant of Jehovah died there in the
land of Moab, according to the word of Jehovah. And he
buried him in the valley in the land of Moab over against
Beth-peor: but no man knoweth of his sepulchre unto
this day. And Moses was a hundred and twenty years old
when he died: his eye was not dim, nor his natural force
abated (Deut. 34:5-7).

CHAPTER VII

Joshua

The Book of Joshua

WHAT SORT OF COUNTRY was the land of Canaan, toward which the Children of Israel looked so longingly throughout the days of the wilderness wanderings? To Moses it had been revealed as a land "flowing with milk and honey" (Exod. 3:8). It was indeed a fruitful country, lying along the Arabian shore of the Mediterranean and forming the western end of that rich tract of land known as the Fertile Crescent. To the south lay the Sinai peninsula and Egypt, to the north, Babylonia; on the west and east respectively were the Mediterranean Sea and Arabia. Canaan covered only a small area, being approximately one hundred and fifty miles from north to south—and about one hundred miles from east to west at its widest point.

The chief value of Canaan's location was that it was the passageway between Babylonia and Egypt. Living there the Hebrews came in contact with the people of the foremost countries of the civilized ancient world, and while this tended to broaden their minds, it presented definite hazards to a people dedicated to the service of God.

Many nations called Canaan their homeland. On the coast to the north were the Phoenicians, whose land the Hebrews never attempted to occupy. To the south, likewise on the coast, were the Philistines

who, in the days of Joshua, were not a powerful
people. In the interior were the Canaanites, the
Amorites, Hittites, Girgashites, Perizzites, and several smaller tribes, such as the Jebusites who held
the territory around Jebus, the site of which later
became the city of Jerusalem. Surrounding Canaan
proper was a chain of kingdoms, the Syrians or
Aramaeans to the northeast and the Edomites,
Moabites, and Ammonites, peoples akin to the Hebrews, to the south and southeast.

The Book of Joshua is primarily a book of
prophetic teaching. Its historical value is secondary.
It presents a somewhat idealized account of the conquest of Canaan under the leadership of Joshua,
Moses' successor. However, the book is rich in spiritual significance. The name Joshua means "Jehovah is salvation" (M.D. 368) which is the same
as Jesus, the Greek form of the Hebrew Joshua.
Joshua is often referred to as a type of Christ, though
in Joshua we do not find the full spiritual realization typified by Jesus. There is in Joshua, however,
a conscious realization of identity with Jehovah and
the courage to act in accord with His will.

The Promised Land represents the good that
God has for every man. It signifies spiritual realization and also the outer blessings that come into the
life of the one who functions in harmony with the
I AM or spiritual self. We enter the Promised Land
with the Joshua quality in charge. This is told by
the events that took place when Joshua assumed
leadership of the Israelites. "Jehovah spake unto

Joshua the son of Nun, Moses' minister" (Josh.
1:1). We are never aware of the Lord speaking to
us until we are in a receptive frame of mind. This
comes as the result of prayer and we, like Joshua,
receive guidance and assurance:

Moses my servant is dead; now therefore arise, go
over this Jordan, thou, and all this people, unto the land
which I do give to them, even to the children of Israel.
. . . There shall not any man be able to stand before thee
all the days of thy life: as I was with Moses, so I will be
with thee; I will not fail thee, nor forsake thee. Be strong
and of good courage; for thou shalt cause this people to
inherit the land which I sware unto their fathers to give
them. Only be strong and very courageous, to observe
to do according to all the law . . . turn not from it to the
right hand or to the left, that thou mayest have good success whithersoever thou goest (Josh. 1:2-7).

Even though we may see the Promised Land, or
the good, before us there are difficulties to overcome
ere we take possession of it. There is no gain except
as we put forth effort. We need to be strong and
very courageous and, above all else, to remember
that God is with us. The first task to confront Joshua
was to cross the Jordan River. Before attempting to
do so, Joshua sent two spies into Jericho, the city
directly across the river, to ascertain its strength.
There the spies found a woman who was in sympathy
with the Israelites. She was Rahab, a harlot. The
spies lodged in her house, and the king of Jericho,
discovering they were there, sent messengers to take
them prisoner. Rahab hid the spies on the roof of
her house and told the King's messengers they had

departed. "Pursue after them quickly; for ye will overtake them" (Josh. 2:5), she said. When the messengers had gone, Rahab confided to the spies that she knew their God was all-powerful and that He had given the land to the Hebrews.

Then she let them down by a cord through the window; for her house was upon the side of the wall, and she dwelt upon the wall. And she said unto them, Get you to the mountain, lest the pursuers light upon you; and hide yourselves there three days, until the pursuers be returned; and afterwards may ye go your way (Josh. 2:15, 16).

A dramatic touch in the narrative is that, before the spies returned to the Hebrew camp, they gave back to Rahab the scarlet cord she had used in letting them down the wall, and told her that when the Hebrews took the city she was to place the cord in her window and it would be a sign to Joshua's soldiers to save her home.

After the Israelites settled in Canaan, Rahab married Salmon, a Hebrew. From them was descended Boaz, who became the husband of Ruth, and David and Jesus were thus of Rahab's line. Charles Fillmore states that Rahab represents "the natural love in man, with the fidelity and faithfulness of that love, which, becoming centered on spiritual things, opens the way for man to enter into the Promised Land" (M.D. 543). As a harlot she "signifies the depths of sense into which the natural love had fallen. Yet when the city was approached by the spies (first thoughts of Truth . . .) this natural love at once recognized the superiority of spiritual ideas over the old carnal beliefs, and so received gladly the new light. This love therefore is preserved and is lifted to higher expression."

Rahab also rendered a great service by telling Joshua's spies that the people of Jericho feared the Israelites, and the spies reported to him: "Truly Jehovah hath delivered into our hands all the land; and moreover all the inhabitants of the land do melt away before us" (Josh. 2:24). Actually the men of Jericho were defeated by their own fears even before Joshua reached the city.

And Joshua rose up early in the morning; and they removed from Shittim, and came to the Jordan, he and all the children of Israel; and they lodged there before they passed over. . . . And Joshua said unto the people, Sanctify yourselves; for to-morrow Jehovah will do wonders among you (Josh. 3:1, 5).

The Jordan represents the barrier, whatever it may be, between ourselves and our good. When we come to the Jordan and are willing to pass over it, it means we have reached the state of mind in which we have the courage to face our problems, cleanse from mind the negative beliefs, and fearlessly follow the guidance of Spirit. The priests who carried the Ark of the Covenant signify dominant spiritual ideas in consciousness. They stood in the water; that is, they began the task at hand in faith. We would often like for the waters to part beforehand, but the work of faith must go forward before there is any evidence of the outworking of a problem.

Let Joshua (saviour) instruct the priests (strong
spiritual thoughts in consciousness) to go forward
and stand guard, and we shall see the parting of the
waters (difficulty) and shall pass through in safety.

When Abraham entered Canaan from Babylonia, centuries before the time of Joshua, he made
no attempt to conquer the various peoples who occupied the land. Instead he lived among them, moving from place to place to suit his own needs or
when the inhabitants became unfriendly. Throughout the Patriarchal period the Hebrews lived a
nomadic life. They were shepherds and small in
number, but during the time they lived in Egypt
their numbers increased. When they entered Canaan
under Joshua's leadership it was with the idea of
taking the land for themselves.

Joshua's first task was to overthrow the city of
Jericho, as it was directly in the Hebrews' line of
march. It was a walled city, and the Hebrews had no
implements of war. Joshua resorted to ingenious
means. Seven priests were instructed to walk before
the Ark of the Covenant bearing seven trumpets of
rams' horns, followed by the men of war. Once a
day for six days the procession marched around the
city. On the seventh day they marched seven times,
and when the priests blew the trumpets, all the
men of war shouted with a mighty shout. The walls
of Jericho came tumbling down.

Are not spiritual victories often won by means
that seem utterly foolish and inadequate to human
reason? As Paul so aptly said, "The foolishness of

God is wiser than men . . . but God chose the foolish things of the world, that he might put to shame them that are wise" (I Cor. 1:25, 27). No matter how impossible a task seems from the mortal point of view, if we go at it under divine guidance we shall succeed. There are conditions that seem like impregnable fortresses, such as Jericho, and we cannot break them down by force no matter how hard we try. However, they crumble with very little physical effort on our part when we listen for and obey instructions from on high.

Great was the rejoicing of the Children of Israel when Jericho fell. We are always highly elated when an overcoming is made and then we feel so confident of spiritual power we are apt to think we can quickly vanquish any problem that comes. But all too soon defeat follows victory. This is because the whole consciousness has not been redeemed. There are still qualities within us that must be lifted up. The Biblical narrative relates that in attempting to take the Amorite city of Ai many of the Israelites were slain and the remainder returned to their camp in despair. "The hearts of the people melted, and became as water" (Josh. 7:5). Joshua prayed, and it was revealed to him that the Hebrews' defeat was due to wickedness among his own people.

Upon investigation Joshua discovered that one of the Hebrew soldiers, Achan, had disobeyed the command of the Lord. At Jericho the Israelites had been warned not to keep any of the spoils for themselves. These were to be consecrated unto the Lord, and were to "come into the treasury of Jehovah" (Josh. 6:19). Achan had taken for himself a "goodly Babylonish mantle, and two hundred shekels of silver, and a wedge of gold of fifty shekels weight" (Josh. 7:21).

The name Achan means "troubler" (M.D. 20), and the man bearing it represents covetousness. When this quality is active in consciousness it always brings trouble and sorrow. Achan, being an Israelite, symbolizes a certain degree of spiritual awareness that knows better than to yield to temptation. In our present state of development we all have something of Achan in us, and at times we let our selfish desires for what seems good on the material plane obscure our spiritual vision. Then, like Achan, we try to hide our sin and are as unsuccessful as he was.

If we read this account literally, it seems unreasonably harsh that Achan and all his family were stoned to death. Spiritually, however, it tells us that our consciousness must be entirely free of what Achan represents: greed. "Every tree that bringeth not forth good fruit is hewn down, and cast into the fire" (Matt. 7:19). When Achan and his family were no longer in their midst the Hebrews attacked Ai and conquered it.

Under Joshua's leadership the conquest of Canaan progressed. A tribe called the Gibeonites made peace with Joshua, and because of this they were attacked by several other tribes. The Gibeonites called upon Joshua for assistance. The combined tribes warring against them were larger than the forces of Joshua and the Gibeonites, but Joshua received the divine assurance, "Fear them not: for I have delivered them into thy hands" (Josh. 10:8). When we work with God, victory is assured. We must realize this before we can go forth in faith.

As the battle progressed, Joshua was winning, but it seemed to him that night would surely fall before the victory was complete. And Joshua cried:

Sun, stand thou still upon Gibeon;
And thou, Moon, in the valley of Aijalon.
And the sun stood still, and the moon stayed,
Until the nation had avenged themselves of their enemies. . . .
And there was no day like that before it or after it, that Jehovah hearkened unto the voice of a man: for Jehovah fought for Israel (Josh. 10:12-14).

This poem was one of the popular songs of Israel and belonged to a very ancient period before there were any written records. Undoubtedly it has lived because of the spiritual idea in it. God will give us opportunity to complete all that we need to do. And when we work in harmony with Him there is always sufficient time to finish our task. In the busy lives we lead, time is often at a premium, and we cry, "Sun, stand thou still." If our prayer is directed to God, we shall have such order and efficiency in the performance of our work that we accomplish more in a shorter time.

There is also another spiritual idea conveyed by

this passage. "And the sun stood still, and the moon stayed," and the wind and storm obeyed the voice of Jesus. Spiritual man is master even of the elements, and in the realization of divine order in us and in our affairs it is manifested at our word.

Chapters 13 and 14 of The Book of Joshua record the division of the land among the twelve tribes. There were actually thirteen tribes, for each of the sons of Joseph—Ephraim and Manasseh— was recognized as the father of a tribe. However, Levi, the priestly tribe, received no allotment of land. Instead, each tribe gave certain cities to the Levites. Reuben, Gad, and half the tribe of Manasseh had asked for and received land in Gilead. Among the others, Judah, Ephraim, and the other half of Manasseh were given their choice. The remaining seven tribes drew lots.

The twelve tribes of Israel represent the twelve spiritual faculties of man. When we start our spiritual unfoldment these faculties are quickened, although they do not come into full expression until the Christ consciousness is attained. In the Joshua stage of development, each is assigned its rightful sphere of activity, symbolized by dividing the land among the twelve tribes. Each has its separate place but should function in harmony with the others. The tribes were to be independent and yet interdependent. This was Joshua's wise plan for them. The fact that they soon began to drift apart and live unto themselves was not the fault of the great leader, who understood that every tribe should have its own portion of land, though all should remain one people.

It is important that we understand the function of each of our spiritual faculties as separate and also as part of the whole. Ephraim (will) has its individual function but should operate in conjunction with Manasseh (understanding). Reuben (discernment) should ever co-operate with Benjamin (faith). Levi, who represents love, was placed among all the tribes, as love in individual consciousness has a vital part to play in the unfolding of each other spiritual quality.

As the Hebrews gave up their nomadic habits after moving into Canaan and gradually became accustomed to an agricultural life, they tended to adopt the religious beliefs and practices of the native people. Baalism was the religion of Canaan. The Baalim were nature gods who were worshiped in an effort to insure the fertility of the land. At the groves and high places the most licentious rites were performed, especially at the three annual festivals of spring, summer, and autumn. The gods were cajoled or placated by sacrifice, often of human beings. Baalism was a primitive form of religion in which moral and spiritual teaching was wholly absent. Every great Hebrew leader and prophet protested the worship of such gods and endeavored to instill in the Israelites a love for the true God who had led them forth from bondage and who required obedience and righteousness of them. Against Baal worship Joshua warned his people most emphatically in his last days:

Now therefore fear Jehovah, and serve him in sincerity
and in truth . . . And if it seem evil unto you to serve
Jehovah, choose you this day whom ye will serve . . . but
as for me and my house, we will serve Jehovah (Josh.
24:14, 15).

Joshua wanted the Children of Israel to put the
Lord first. This is fundamental to true progress. It
is, however, easier to worship a god who requires
material gifts than one who asks obedience to his
commandments. Each of us has to decide whom he
will serve. Only the Lord is mighty to open His hand
and satisfy the desire of every living thing.

As we develop spiritually each God-given quality
unfolds, knows fullness, and then moves into the
background of consciousness. This does not mean
that the work of any quality is no longer needed,
but merely that it is time to let another come forth.
Joshua's mission was to lead the Children of Israel
into the Promised Land. Before they could take full
possession of the Promised Land, other characters,
representing other qualities, had to assume control.
This transition is represented in the Bible by the
passing of one leader and the rise of another.

And it came to pass after these things, that Joshua the
son of Nun, the servant of Jehovah, died, being a hundred and ten years old. And they buried him in the border
of his inheritance . . . which is in the hill-country of
Ephraim (Josh. 24:29, 30).

CHAPTER VIII

The Judges and Samuel

Judges; I Samuel 1-16:13

THE OPENING WORDS of The Book of Judges gives evidence that all Canaan had not been conquered under Joshua. Though the entire land had been apportioned to the twelve tribes, they were not actually in possession of the territory allotted to them. Their greatest weakness lay in their inability to work together. Each tribe showed a tendency to confine itself to its own interests. Anarchy reigned to a large degree, for "every man did that which was right in his own eyes" (Judg. 17:6). A human standard is not sufficient; it overlooks the rights and needs of others. The Hebrews had not yet discovered that only in unity is there strength, and though each tribe fought valiantly to drive out the enemy, it was often unsuccessful. Sometimes there was fighting among the Hebrews.

In attempting to take the land that they believed to be theirs by the will of Jehovah, the Hebrews came near to forgetting Jehovah Himself. Joshua had warned them to shun the gods of the Canaanites, but there soon developed a strong tendency to worship the Baalim and Ashtaroth and even to intermarry with the Canaanites.

During this period of about a century the Hebrews were ruled by chieftains called judges. When a tribe was forced to war it selected its ablest soldier as leader and generally retained him as civil ruler afterward. The rule of twelve such judges is recorded in The Book of Judges. Some of them were far from being worthy. Each, however, made some contribution to the unification of the Hebrew tribes. When a particularly strong enemy attacked one group, the leader of that tribe would call on one or more other tribes to join with him in fighting. This was a step in the right direction and laid the foundation for the later unification of the tribes brought about in part by Saul and fully by David.

Four of the judges deserve special mention. The first was Deborah. Deborah was the only woman judge and she symbolizes the attribute of discrimination (M.D. 168). Barak was the warrior that Deborah called to fight against the Canaanites. Barak represents the will.

When the inner intuitive judgment [Deborah] and the directive power in understanding [Barak] are rightly joined, victory over the enemies of the Children of Israel follows. The Children of Israel represent the real, enduring spiritual thoughts, and the enemies are the material, transitory thoughts. Barak (the executiveness of the will), the general of the armies of Israel, should not go into action without good judgment (Deborah). The only way to overcome the opposition of the adverse thought realm is to understand the law and to keep constantly unified with judgment based upon inner discrimination. This is represented by Deborah's accompanying Barak to battle. The victory belongs to the intuitive judgment, and not to the will (M.D. 168).

Gideon, the next judge of note, subdued the

Midianites. The stories of Gideon, found in Judges 6:11—8:33, are filled with splendid spiritual lessons for us. The name Gideon means "destroyer" (M.D. 233) and he represents denial, a most important practice in the overcoming of erroneous states of mind (enemies).

The enemy against whom Gideon waged war was Midian, which means *strife* or *contention*. To many people there is no other enemy that is so difficult to kill. Petty quarrels, jealousies, uncharitable thoughts—how they come back again and again! They can never be overcome except by positive denial made in the realization that no error has any power or reality of itself. This form of denial, with an assurance of the power and love of God, will overcome all strife. The Midianites must be exterminated before we can possess the Promised Land in its entirety. We must "smite the Midianites as one man," as impersonal evil, and consider even that as a claim that never was and never shall be (M.D. 234).

Jephthah was the third of the outstanding judges. Charles Fillmore states that Jephthah represents:

A very influential thought in the judgment faculty in man. Though cast out as evil by the more formal, established religious thoughts (his brethren), and denied inheritance with them, this Jephthah thought persists in holding to the good, to perfection. . . . Through Jehovah, the I AM . . . the Jephthah thought becomes first a deliverer and then a judge of Israel (the true religious and spiritual thoughts of the consciousness). It even takes precedence over its brothers . . . So Jephthah, this ruling thought, having been given authority, leads the Israelites (true thoughts) to victory over the Ammonites (impure, ignorant, and disorderly thoughts), the soul is established in purity and Truth, and the land (body) has peace (M.D. 337).

The fourth of the greater judges was Samson. At that time the Philistines were menacing the Hebrews, and though Samson's great desire was to conquer them, he let himself be betrayed by yielding to unredeemed forces in his own being. Sacrificing his ideals, he sacrificed himself. His life stands as a warning of how our strength and ability may be depleted when we do not keep ourselves in harmony with Spirit.

The life of Samson, as given in Judges, represents the different movements of strength in human consciousness, and its betrayal and end. Samson did all kinds of athletic stunts, but was finally robbed of his strength by Delilah, a Philistine woman, who had his head shaved while he slept on her knees. Hair represents vitality. When the vital principle is taken away the strength goes with it. This weakens the body and it finally perishes. . . .

The destruction of Samson and his enemies pictures the activity of strength independent of divine law. Ideas of strength must be established in substance and expressed in judgment before they will act constructively in the organism and preserve the body (M.D. 570).

From a spiritual point of view this entire period reveals the fluctuation in consciousness of one who has recognized the presence of the Lord but finds it well nigh impossible to remain faithful to Him. When Joshua counseled his people to worship the true God, they stoutly affirmed, "Far be it from us that we should forsake Jehovah, to serve other gods" (Josh. 24:16). However, all of us discover that though the spirit is willing the flesh is indeed weak. Outer pressure is apt to focus our attention on outer conditions, until after a time we lose the feeling that God is real and we, too, find it easy to disregard Him. But in making even slight progress on the spiritual path we gain something of enduring value. It may be obscured for a time and appear to be lost (as is indicated in the last chapters of The Book of Judges, which relate the confusion of divided worship and interests in the ranks of the Hebrew tribes), but it will rise again and prepare the way for additional enlightenment and strength. This is shown in our Bible narrative by the rule of the last and greatest of the judges, Samuel.

Samuel was a child of promise, like Isaac, Samson, and John the Baptist. His mother Hannah prayed for a son, and even before his birth she dedicated him to God's service. Eli was the judge and priest of Israel at the time Samuel was born, and when he was quite young his mother Hannah took him to Shiloh and placed him in Eli's care. The name Samuel means "instructed of God" (M.D. 571), and he represents spiritual receptivity, and also judgment. Both of these qualities are prominent in the life of Samuel. Spiritual receptivity develops first; without it there can be no spiritual judgment.

At an early age Samuel proved his willingness to listen to the Lord:

And the child Samuel ministered unto Jehovah before Eli. And the word of Jehovah was precious in those days; there was no frequent vision. And it came to pass at that time, when Eli was laid down in his place . . . and the lamp of God was not yet gone out, and Samuel was laid down *to sleep,* in the temple of Jehovah, where the ark of God was; that Jehovah called Samuel: and he said, Here am I (I Sam. 3:1-4).

Samuel thought that it was Eli who called him, but Eli said, "I called not, my son; lie down again." Three times the Lord spoke, and "Eli perceived that Jehovah had called the child" and told Samuel to answer if he were called again. "And Jehovah came, and stood, and called as at other times, Samuel, Samuel. Then Samuel said, Speak; for thy servant heareth" (I Sam. 3:10).

God speaks to us continually, but many times our attention is so given to the outer that we do not hear. We have to serve in the temple (worship) willingly and obediently before the voice of God can arouse us from the sleep of materiality. Then we must listen to what He has to say. We talk a great deal to God but rarely let His words reach us. In conversations with people, we speak and then listen, but far too often ours is a one-sided conversation with the Lord. He will always direct us if we will listen. The most potent part of the silence is not our prayer but the stillness into which we move that we may hear what God would say to us. We should ask for ears so attuned to Spirit that we can hear the divine voice and hearing, heed.

The Lord had an important message for Samuel. He revealed that Samuel was to be the next judge of Israel, for he was more worthy than the sons of

Eli. Eli symbolizes the intellect reaching toward God but deterred by mortal thoughts. This state of consciousness must be replaced by Samuel, who is eager to be instructed by the Lord.

Because Samuel was receptive, the faculty of spiritual judgment grew apace. The chief foes of the Hebrews were the Philistines, who, better armed and organized, were making great inroads upon Israelite territory. Once the Hebrews were so near to defeat that they sent to Shiloh for the Ark of the Covenant. The Ark of the Covenant plays an important part in Hebrew history, and what it represents is vital to our spiritual unfoldment. It symbolizes:

> The original spark of divinity in man's being. It is a covenant, or agreement, of the Father with the son that he shall inherit all that the Father has. . . .
> This original spiritual spark is a very sacred, holy thing, because upon its development depends man's immortality. It is represented as occupying the most holy place in the temple and as being protected and cared for with great devotion. All that man is has been brought forth from this central spark, yet the sense-conscious man often neglects it and ignores its very existence (M.D. 64).

At the time of Samuel, the Ark of the Covenant was kept in the sanctuary at Shiloh (since the Temple at Jerusalem had not yet been built). The Hebrews' sending for the Ark to be with them in battle is symbolic of our desire for divine protection.

Great was the consternation of the Hebrews when the Ark of the Covenant was captured by the Philistines. Deprived of what they considered spiritual support they were ignominiously defeated. They did not have sufficient understanding to discern that spiritual power was not in the Ark itself but in what it represented. People often mistake the symbol for the reality. Our religious institutions as such cannot save us. They stand as symbols of the presence of God, but we have to contact that presence through prayer before we can "abide under the shadow of the Almighty" (Psalms 91:1). The Ark was of no benefit to the Philistines; on the contrary, it proved to be a curse, and after a time the Ark was returned to the Hebrews. The Philistines had no conception of its spiritual significance, and therefore, the Ark was without value to them.

More than the physical presence of the Ark of the Covenant was needed to protect Israel. Samuel, representing spiritual judgment, understood this. Calling the people together he said to them:

> If ye do return unto Jehovah with all your heart, then put away the foreign gods and the Ashtaroth from among you, and direct your hearts unto Jehovah, and serve him only; and he will deliver you out of the hand of the Philistines (I Sam. 7:3).

Perhaps the Israelites were laboring under the mistaken idea that if one God was good, several gods might be better. "But one thing is needful" (Luke 10:42) and this Samuel encouraged them to do: "Return unto Jehovah with all your heart" (I Sam. 7:3).

The Children of Israel heeded the advice of Samuel. They put aside the images of heathen gods and gathered at Mizpah to fast and pray. We have to prepare ourselves to receive good of the Lord and we do it in just this way; that is, by turning to Him, casting aside heathen or unregenerate thoughts, and praying. In this way only can we generate spiritual strength.

While the Hebrews were gathered at Mizpah word was brought that the Philistines were planning to attack them. Instead of scattering in an effort to protect themselves, they asked of Samuel, "Cease not to cry unto Jehovah our God for us, that he will save us out of the hand of the Philistines" (I Sam. 7:8). In a prayerful consciousness and putting their entire dependence upon the Lord, the Hebrews met and defeated the Philistine host.

When Samuel grew old he appointed his sons to judge Israel. Now "his sons walked not in his ways, but turned aside after lucre, and took bribes, and perverted justice" (I Sam. 8:3). The elders of Israel demanded a king, "like all the nations" (I Sam. 8:5). To this Samuel objected, pointing out the trials that would come to them at the hands of a despotic monarch. To Samuel the real ruler of all Israel was Jehovah. But the people answered, "Nay; but we will have a king over us, that we also may be like all the nations, and that our king may judge us, and go out before us, and fight our battles" (I Sam. 8:19, 20). Samuel asked for divine guidance, "And Jehovah said to Samuel, Hearken unto their voice, and make them a king" (I Sam. 8:22).

Samuel thus served as a connecting link between

two periods of Hebrew history, the period of the judges and the period of the kings. His choice of a king fell upon a man named Saul, of the tribe of Benjamin, "a young man and a goodly: and there was not among the children of Israel a goodlier person than he: from his shoulders and upward he was higher than any of the people" (I Sam. 9:2).

Saul signifies personal will. He represents the consciousness in its natural estate. It is willful and stubborn, shy and impulsive, yet very brave under great stress. When first chosen as king Saul was very humble; and true humility is one of the first qualifications for spiritual leadership (M.D. 576).

In the early part of his reign Saul lived up to the best expectations of Samuel. Later he became arbitrary and disobedient. Unless the will (Saul) is under divine guidance it becomes a destructive force. The highest function of our will is to execute God's commands. When we will do His will, this faculty is a mighty power for good, but in the determination to have what we want when we want it, we move farther and farther from the Lord and bring a vast amount of trouble upon ourselves. Saul is typical of the person who begins a great task with true humility of spirit and accomplishes much, then gradually lets selfishness rule the will and becomes dictatorial and even cruel. This separates him from the divine or higher impulses within and starts a decline that ends in loss and final defeat.

This deterioration is borne out in the life of Saul. It was Samuel's responsibility to offer sacrifices to

Jehovah, but when Samuel was delayed in appearing at Gilgal for this purpose, Saul impatiently performed the ceremony.

And Samuel said to Saul, Thou hast done foolishly; thou hast not kept the commandment of Jehovah thy God, which he commanded thee: for now would Jehovah have established thy kingdom upon Israel for ever (I Sam. 13:13).

Samuel then prophesied that the kingdom would be taken from Saul.

Later Samuel directed Saul to wage war on the Amalekites and utterly destroy them. Instead Saul spared Agag, the king of Amalek, and kept the best of the spoils of battle. When called to account by Samuel, Saul denied that he had disobeyed and said that it was the people who took the spoils for sacrifice to Jehovah. Impatience, disobedience, and falsehood accompany the exercise of the will bent on doing its way.

And Samuel said, Hath Jehovah as great delight in burnt-offerings and sacrifices, as in obeying the voice of Jehovah? Behold, to obey is better than sacrifice, and to hearken than the fat of rams. . . . Because thou hast rejected the word of Jehovah, he hath also rejected thee from being king (I Sam. 15:22, 23).

Was the Lord unmerciful in demanding that the Amalekites be slain to the last man? Spiritually interpreted it becomes evident why Samuel was insistent that Saul, in falling short of complete obedience, had displeased Jehovah. The name Amalek

means "warlike" or "valley dweller," and the
Amalekites represent "the base desires of the individual" (M.D. 43).

To those in spiritual understanding it is clear that the
vale *(valley dweller)* represents that great realm of mind
called the subconscious. The Amalekites symbolize the
animal forces, appetites, and passions. They are *warlike,*
and are destructive in their nature. They must be cleansed
completely out of consciousness by denial.

Disobedience has many forms; the most stubborn is
that which absolutely refuses to obey. It stands up for its
rights. It tells us that certain things are good for us, that
the race has always indulged in them, and that such in-
dulgence is necessary. Such ideas as these are the Amalekites
down in the vale. They have become fixed in consciousness and refuse to abdicate. They are not receptive to the
illumination of Spirit; they crave self-gratification and are
determined to have it. They must be taken up in prayer
and denied place in consciousness. If we do not destroy
these errors that God commands us to destroy, sooner or
later they will obtain command to such an extent that they
will endeavor to destroy us (M.D. 43).

Samuel mourned over Saul's failure to rule
righteously (as we sometimes grieve over a plan that
does not work out as we thought and hoped). For
this the Lord rebuked Samuel and told him to go to
Jesse the Bethlehemite adding, "I have provided
me a king among his sons" (I Sam. 16:1). There is
always something that can be done, another way
of solving a difficulty. It takes spiritual judgment to
perceive it. Samuel went to Bethlehem and called
Jesse and his sons to him. Samuel would have selected Eliab, the first of Jesse's sons.

But Jehovah said unto Samuel, Look not on his countenance, or on the height of his stature; because I have rejected him: for *Jehovah seeth* not as man seeth; for man looketh on the outward appearance, but Jehovah looketh on the heart (I Sam. 16:7).

Seven of Jesse's sons were presented to Samuel, but he knew that Jehovah had chosen none of them. When plans are presented to us we are apt to be too quick in making a decision. It is well to be still and listen for inner guidance. "Are here all thy children?" Samuel asked of Jesse.

And he said, There remaineth yet the youngest, and, behold, he is keeping the sheep. And Samuel said unto Jesse, Send and fetch him; for we will not sit down till he come hither. And he sent, and brought him [David] in. Now he was ruddy, and withal of a beautiful countenance, and goodly to look upon. And Jehovah said, Arise, anoint him; for this is he (I Sam. 16:11, 12).

All the days of his life Samuel never varied in his allegiance to the Lord, and the truths that he received he shared with his fellow men. He held a place of honor among the Israelites of his day, and the spiritual qualities of receptivity and judgment, which he represents, are precious to us today. As we pray may we, too, say to our Lord, "Speak; for thy servant heareth" (I Sam. 3:10).

CHAPTER IX

David

I Samuel 16:14; II Samuel 1-24;
I Chronicles 10-29

D AVID, THE YOUTH whom Samuel anointed
king, was to prove his fitness to reign over
Israel. We are told that "the Spirit of Jehovah came mightily upon David from that day forward" (I Sam. 16:13). The name David means "beloved," and David "represents divine love indi-
vidualized in human consciousness" (M. D. 166).
This quality, love, in its highest expression always
serves, and David's life reveals service to God and to
his people. In its lowest form love is selfish and
sometimes vicious, and this undesirable expression
of love is also evidenced in David's life. However,
the higher development of love is more often
prominent, and long after David's reign the Bible
records that the Lord bestowed certain blessings
on his descendants, "for David my servant's sake"
(I Kings 11:13). God is love, and we come nearest
to Him when this quality is in the foreground of
consciousness.

Our first acquaintance with David after his
anointing is when he was sent to play on the harp
for Saul. An *"evil* spirit" troubled the King, and
music then, as now, "hath charms to soothe the savage breast." In Robert Browning's superb dramatic
poem "Saul," there is a scene where David is playing

for Saul in an effort to win him from madness. To his music David added prayer, and there came to him a great realization of the power of the Almighty to answer the prayers of men. And Browning has David exclaim:

"I believe it! 'Tis Thou, God, that givest, 'tis I who
    receive:
 In the first is the last, in Thy will is my power to believe.
 All's one gift: Thou canst grant it moreover, as prompt
    to my prayer
 As I breathe out this breath, as I open these arms to the
    air."

Surely this faith was with David throughout his eventful life. It was evidenced in his conflict with Goliath, the Philistine giant. The Philistines were the strongest foe of Israel, and King Saul was hard pressed in his battle with them. Goliath challenged any Israelite soldier to combat: "I defy the armies of Israel this day; give me a man, that we may fight together. And when Saul and all Israel heard those words of the Philistine, they were dismayed, and greatly afraid" (I Sam. 17:10, 11). But David, who had come to the camp of the Hebrews to bring gifts of food to his brothers in Saul's army, heard of the challenge and said to the King, "Let no man's heart fail because of him [Goliath]; thy servant will go and fight with this Philistine" (I Sam. 17:32). And so he did. His words to Goliath are significant:

Thou comest to me with a sword, and with a spear, and with a javelin: but I come to thee in the name of Jehovah of hosts, the God of the armies of Israel, whom thou hast defied. This day will Jehovah deliver thee into

my hand . . . that all this assembly may know that Jehovah saveth not with sword and spear; for the battle is
Jehovah's, and he will give you into our hand (I Sam.
17:45-47).

Out he went against the giant with a slingshot
and a stone, and when the stone sank into Goliath's
forehead and he fell, David cut off Goliath's head
with the man's own sword. Here again the idea is
that the one who depends on God always prevails if
his cause be right and just. In our own personal experience Goliath represents any huge problem that
looms before us and for which we have no remedy
in the outer. When we meet it in the consciousness
of Immanuel (God with us) it is solved easily and
quickly.

Though David had been anointed as king of Israel, Saul was the actual ruler, and David never attempted to take the kingdom from him. It was to be
years before David became king in fact. At this time
he was a young man, and after the slaying of Goliath
he became a mighty warrior in Saul's army. Great
was the love between Jonathan, the eldest son of
Saul, and David. "The soul of Jonathan was knit
with the soul of David, and Jonathan loved him as
his own soul" (I Sam. 18:1).

Jonathan typifies the soul substance that, in man's unfoldment, tries to unite will and love. He symbolizes that
soul quality which, though the offspring of the will (Saul),
turns yearningly toward love (David). . . . He may be
termed human affection and desire set upon spiritual things,
while David is divine love. These two are closely related
in consciousness (M.D. 362).

This affection was to endure throughout the lives of both men. Jonathan proved his devotion when he saved David's life and by his repeated assertion that David and not he (Jonathan) would inherit the kingdom. David proved this by his grief over the death of Jonathan, and by his kindness years later to Jonathan's lame son Mephibosheth.

Saul also gave his daughter Michal to David for his wife. She protected David against her father when, in anger, Saul would have killed him.

Saul's antagonism toward David was inevitable. When the will operates on the personal plane it becomes jealous of its rights and fearful lest it be deposed from power. Both qualities, will and love, are innate in man, and if he functions in the spiritual consciousness, will and love are harmonious. But Saul (will) had fallen away from Spirit and sought to slay David (love). The mission of love is to serve; will frequently demands to be served. Thus the two are incompatible, and dissension arises quickly, incited by the arrogant will.

The first rift between Saul and David came when Saul grew jealous of the people's admiration for David. Love is a magnet for the attraction of love from others, and when Saul and David returned from battle, the women in the streets cried:

> Saul hath slain his thousands,
> And David his ten thousands
> (I Sam. 18:7).

The King was "very wroth" and pondered,

"What can he have more but the kingdom?" (I Sam. 18:8). From that time on, Saul was intent on slaying David. Will would crush anything that stands in its way. Three times Saul attacked David, and when Jonathan knew that David's life was in danger, he gave David the signal to flee from the King's court.

David retired to the wilderness of Southern Judah, and there he spent a number of years in exile. Gathering together a group of men who were likewise in disfavor with Saul or dissatisfied with his rule, David became the leader of a rebel band. Saul pursued him relentlessly. On two occasions David had opportunity to kill Saul, once in the cave of Engedi where he cut off the skirt of the King's robe (I Samuel 24), and once in the wilderness of Ziph when David slipped into Saul's tent at night and took his spear and a cruse of water (I Samuel 26). Saul was so touched by David's compassion that he invited him to return to the court and called him "my son." However, David had every reason to be skeptical of the King's sincerity and preferred to remain free, though a fugitive.

During his years of exile David experienced a wonderful sense of companionship with God. When we have a true love for our Creator, it is not only in good times that we commune with Him but even more do we seek Him when the situation is a difficult one. In exile (apart from good) we can say:

O God, thou art my God; earnestly will I seek thee:
My soul thirsteth for thee, my flesh longeth for thee,
In a dry and weary land, where no water is.

So have I looked upon thee in the sanctuary,
To see thy power and thy glory.
Because thy lovingkindness is better than life,
My lips shall praise thee

(Psalms 63:1-4).

If we love the Lord, we ask Him to show us the
way also. The phrase is repeated, "David inquired
of Jehovah" (I Sam. 23:2, 4), showing the readiness
with which he turned to God and his desire for divine guidance. We are not freed from a situation by
resistance to it, but by co-operation with Spirit.

Even though David had been anointed by Samuel
as king, he made no attempt to seize the throne. He
considered Saul the lawful ruler and exclaimed,
"Jehovah forbid that I should put forth my hand
against Jehovah's anointed" (I Sam. 26:11).

When we are in the David state of consciousness
we do not violate the dictates of the spiritual, even
though we believe we have a right to some specific
blessing. We wait until the door opens in a natural
way.

Saul's downfall was sure to come. Acting in opposition to the higher impulses of his own nature, he
gradually built disastrous conditions for himself.
Facing another attack by the Philistines, who were
gathered at Shunem, Saul stationed his army in
Gilboa, but he was afraid and "his heart trembled
greatly" (I Sam. 28:5). Saul inquired of Jehovah,
but he had become estranged from the Lord and received no answer. In desperation he went to the
woman of En-dor, a medium, to find out how the

coming battle with the Philistines would terminate. Regarding this Charles Fillmore says:

When we are very anxious to know the future, and slyly seek the so-called wisdom of a medium or clairvoyant, we are under the dominion of wavering human will. When we are sure of our premise in God we do not fear the outcome, and we always know that we shall succeed in every good work; then there is no temptation to go to a fortune teller for advice (M.D. 576).

When the Philistines attacked the Israelites again, this time on Mount Gilboa, three of the sons of Saul were slain, Jonathan among them. Saul, realizing that he would be killed, or taken prisoner, took his own life. David's mourning was deep and sincere. "David's Lament," as it is called, is one of the most beautiful elegies ever written. It begins with the familiar words:
"Thy glory, O Israel, is slain upon thy high places! How are the mighty fallen!" (II Sam. 1:19).

Whenever we plant the right kind of seeds and care for them the harvest is bounteous. David's harvest began with the death of Saul. He was crowned king of Judah at Hebron. For some time the southern tribes had been restive under the rule of Saul and they had no desire to accept Ishbosheth, his son, as king. They much preferred David, who was of the tribe of Judah. Abner, captain of Saul's army, fled with Ishbosheth to Gilead, where the latter was crowned king. Civil war soon broke out, "and David waxed stronger and stronger, but the house of Saul waxed weaker and weaker" (II Sam.

3:1). Finally Abner quarreled with Ishbosheth and joined David. Shortly thereafter, two of Ishbosheth's soldiers killed their king. The murder of Ishbosheth broke the power of the northern kingdom and "all the elders of Israel came to the king to Hebron . . . and they anointed David king over Israel" (II Sam. 5:3). Thus within a period of eight years after Saul's death, David was king over all Israel.

David's great service was in unifying the Hebrew tribes and welding them into a strong kingdom. Love is the co-ordinating, unifying principle of Being, and when one is guided by spiritual love all the forces of his nature are harmonized and strengthened.

David's next move was to select a fitting capital. The town of Jebus in the northern part of Judah was still held by the Jebusites, though the Hebrews had always wanted this particular stronghold. Again David resorted to wisdom, not force. Discovering a gully that led from the town to a spring at the foot of the hill, David marched his men through it and directly into Jebus. The unexpected appearance of the Hebrews so surprised and confused the Jebusites that they offered no resistance. Thus Jerusalem, as Jebus came to be called, grew to be the chief city of the Hebrew nation.

The name Jerusalem means "habitation of peace." Only as we rest in God's peace can we express fully the qualities with which the Almighty has endowed us. Charles Fillmore states that "in man it [Jerusalem] is the abiding consciousness of spiritual peace, which is the result of continuous realizations of spiritual power tempered with spiritual poise and confidence" (M.D. 342).

David then brought the Ark of the Covenant to Jerusalem. When love (David) is active in consciousness, recognition is given to the divine spark within man (Ark of the Covenant) and it is placed in Jerusalem (peace). The Lord then said to David, "Thy house and thy kingdom shall be made sure for ever before thee: thy throne shall be established for ever" (II Sam. 7:16).

For years David had loved and obeyed the Lord and had reaped a great harvest of good. However, David does not represent divine love in full expression, and the time came when David's love was motivated by selfishness. In our own experience our devotion to the Lord may be temporarily obscured by a lustful desire. David's longing for Bathsheba typifies this. When there is a strong sensuous desire in consciousness we scheme to attain its fulfillment regardless of the method used. Bathsheba was the wife of Uriah the Hittite, a soldier in David's army, and David ordered him placed in the front line of battle where he would be slain. "But the thing that David had done displeased Jehovah" (II Sam. 11:27).

Nathan the prophet came to David to bring the King's sin before him. Nathan stands for the spiritual conscience that brings to our attention deviations from God's law of righteousness. Telling David the story of the little ewe lamb that the rich man had taken from the poor one, Nathan aroused David's sense of justice, and the King cried, "The man that hath done this is worthy to die" (II Sam. 12:5). Nathan's reply was, "Thou art the man."

It is easy to make excuses, difficult to face our wrongdoing. But when we are in the David state of consciousness and governed primarily by love in its highest aspect, we are quick to perceive our transgression and sincerely repent:

Have mercy upon me, O God, according to thy loving-
    kindness:
According to the multitude of thy tender mercies blot out
    my transgressions.
Wash me thoroughly from mine iniquity,
And cleanse me from my sin.
           *   *   *
Against thee, thee only, have I sinned,
And done that which is evil in thy sight;
           *   *   *
Behold, thou desirest truth in the inward parts;
And in the hidden part thou wilt make me to know wis-
    dom.
           *   *   *
Create in me a clean heart, O God;
And renew a right spirit within me.
           *   *   *
Restore unto me the joy of thy salvation;
And uphold me with a willing spirit

                       (Psalms 51).

In such repentance a real healing takes place. Though the first child born to David and Bathsheba died, they rejoiced greatly in the birth of a second son, whom they named Solomon.

When our consciousness is not fully redeemed we
continue to meet trying situations, each of which
can be overcome only as we adhere to Truth.
Through the actions of an older son, Absalom,
David encountered one of the greatest sorrows of
his life. Absalom was a handsome, impetuous young
man and a favorite with his father. He represents
"physical beauty without corresponding beauty of
the soul" (M.D. 19).

Absalom's sister Tamar was wronged by her
half brother Amnon, and when David failed to
punish him speedily, Absalom killed Amnon and
fled. After several years in exile, Absalom was restored to the King's favor but, instead of being grateful for this, Absalom began a campaign to under-
mine the people's loyalty to David. He became ambitious for power, even to the point of attempting
to usurp his father's throne. Setting up a revolt at
Hebron, Absalom's forces increased to such numbers that he attacked Jerusalem. David fled the city
and went to Gilead.

Although his distress was great, David still
loved his rebellious son and gave orders that should
his forces defeat those of Absalom the young man's
life was to be spared. He never forgave Joab, the
captain of his host, for slaying Absalom. And when
word was brought to him of his son's death, David
cried, "O my son Absalom, my son, my son Absalom!
would I had died for thee, O Absalom, my son, my
son" (II Sam. 18:33).

David forgot self in his grief over the death of

a wayward son. When we function in the sense consciousness the natural reaction to the downfall of one who has despitefully used us is one of rejoicing or at least a feeling of vindication. But when we attain the place in our development where love rules in the heart, we can forgive those who in ignorance would take what rightfully belongs to us.

King David regained his throne but at the expense of quelling two more revolts, the outgrowth of Absalom's rebellion. There was also a three-year famine that caused great suffering. Hardships are likely to focus our attention on the power of conditions to harm rather than the power of the Lord to bless. David fell into just such a state of consciousness and, becoming fearful, commanded that a census be taken of all the fighting men in the kingdom. Joab objected to this, calling the King's attention to the large increase of men the Lord had given him. Why, asked Joab, should the King delight in numbering them?

From a metaphysical standpoint David's attitude represents the fearful state of consciousness that puts its dependence upon physical might. Like the apostle Thomas, David had to see to believe. "Blessed *are* they that have not seen, and *yet* have believed," said Jesus (John 20:29). Might is not in external force but in the realization that God is the one power. We conquer not by force of arms but by faith in the Lord. David had had proof of this many times in his life and he soon realized his mistake in trusting in his fighting men instead of in the Lord:

And David said unto Jehovah, I have sinned greatly in that which I have done: but now, O Jehovah, put away, I beseech thee, the iniquity of thy servant; for I have done very foolishly (II Sam. 24:10).

A great pestilence swept over the land, causing the death of thousands. David's greatness of spirit is shown in his willingness to take the blame to himself:

And David spake unto Jehovah when he saw the angel that smote the people, and said, Lo, I have sinned, and I have done perversely; but these sheep, what have they done? let thy hand, I pray thee, be against me, and against my father's house (II Sam. 24:17).

Gad the prophet commanded David to rear an altar to the Lord in Jerusalem, "that the plague may be stayed from the people" (II Sam. 24:21). Always the solution to a problem consists of building an altar in consciousness (giving attention to God in prayer). This David did, and the plague was "stayed."

David had it in mind to build a fitting temple for Jehovah in Jerusalem, but this was not to be his privilege. Instead of being resentful of frustrated hopes, the King gathered the material for the temple that the Lord revealed to him would be built by his son Solomon.

Then he called for Solomon his son, and charged him to build a house for Jehovah, the God of Israel. And David said to Solomon his son, As for me, it was in my heart to build a house unto the name of Jehovah my God. But the word of Jehovah came to me, saying, Thou hast shed blood abundantly, and hast made great wars . . . Behold, a son shall be born to thee who shall be a man of rest . . . and I will give peace and quietness unto Israel in his days. He shall build a house for my name . . . Now, my son, Jehovah be with thee; and prosper thou, and build the house of Jehovah thy God, as he hath spoken concerning thee. Only Jehovah give thee discretion and understanding, and give thee charge concerning Israel; that so thou mayest keep the law of Jehovah thy God (I Chron. 22:6-12).

David's work was complete when he unified the kingdom and brought his people together in a closer bond than ever before. This is the function of love, to co-ordinate and harmonize the forces of our being.

And David slept with his fathers, and was buried in the city of David. . . . And Solomon sat upon the throne of David his father; and his kingdom was established greatly (I Kings 2:10).

CHAPTER X

Solomon and the Divided Kingdom

I Kings 1-16; II Chronicles 1-20

A T THE BEGINNING of his reign, Solomon took a lofty view of his responsibilities and chose for himself neither wealth nor honor but the ability to govern his people wisely. His prayer was, "Give thy servant therefore an understanding heart to judge thy people, that I may discern between good and evil" (I Kings 3:9).

And the speech pleased the Lord . . . And God said unto him, Because thou hast asked this thing . . . behold, I have done according to thy word: lo, I have given thee a wise and an understanding heart . . . And I have also given thee that which thou hast not asked, both riches and honor, so that there shall not be any among the kings like unto thee, all thy days. And if thou wilt walk in my ways, to keep my statutes and my commandments, as thy father David did walk, then I will lengthen thy days (I Kings 3:10-14).

When we pray for wisdom to serve well, our desire pleases the Lord; that is, we are in tune with His will for good. Therefore, we have the vision, the strength, and the substance with which to work. All outer conditions were in Solomon's favor, for David had not only unified the kingdom but had extended its boundaries in all directions. True to the charge given him by his father, Solomon started building the Temple.

Spiritually the Temple represents the high consciousness built in us through our devotion to God, our prayers, our efforts to live in harmony with Him. With every thought of Truth we think, with every word of Truth we speak, we are building a house unto Jehovah. It is recorded that when the Ark of the Covenant was brought into the Temple, "the cloud filled the house of Jehovah, so that the priests could not stand to minister by reason of the cloud; for the glory of Jehovah filled the house of Jehovah" (I Kings 8:10, 11). The radiant cloud symbolizes the light that floods our being when we enter "the secret place of the Most High" (Psalms 91:1).

Solomon's next undertaking was the improvement of his capital. In the time of David Jerusalem was little more than a fortress. Solomon made it a great and imposing city, ranking well with the other capitals of the tenth century B.C. He also did much to develop the resources of his kingdom, principally by encouraging trade with other nations. He negotiated successfully with neighboring rulers and put Israel on favorable terms with larger countries. The Hebrew kingdom reached its highest peak under him, and Solomon's fame spread far and wide.

The name Solomon means "whole, complete, peace." Metaphysically it represents "the state of mind that is established in consciousness when the soul is unified with wisdom and love" (M.D. 625).

The results of such a state of consciousness were prominent in the early years of Solomon's reign. However, to acquire a spiritual state of mind in which wisdom and love predominate is one thing; to keep it is quite another. Anyone who aspires to be wise and prays earnestly for wisdom grows in spiritual consciousness. Yet eternal vigilance is necessary to sustain this growth.

Evidently Solomon failed to "pray without ceasing" (I Thess. 5:17). We cannot keep active any attribute of God without caring for it. We may have acquired wisdom or love or peace as a result of prayer, but unless we maintain the prayerful state of mind through which these qualities can function, they recede. And others, unlike them, take their place in mind. Outer interests began to crowd into Solomon's life, and they tended to crowd out the spiritual desire that had once been his. As disobedience and jealousy gradually undermined the fine character of Saul, so ambition and apostasy took their toll of Solomon.

To keep pace with his ambitious projects, the King needed vast sums of money. He raised it by laying burdensome taxes on the people. He enslaved the various foreign inhabitants living in Israel, descendants of the nations who had once occupied the land, and forced the lower class of Hebrews to work for the government certain periods of time each year. As a result of these unjust measures, discontent began to brew within the realm.

In religion Solomon drifted farther and farther from the Lord. His devotion to Jehovah was overshadowed by his love for "many foreign women," foreign princesses, some of whom he married from choice, others in order to make advantageous alliances with neighboring kings.

It came to pass . . . that his wives turned away his heart after other gods; and his heart was not perfect with Jehovah his God, as was the heart of David his father (I Kings 11:4).

When we begin to love the things of the sense plane there is a definite departure in consciousness from spiritual ideals. To please some of his wives, Solomon permitted the erection of altars to heathen gods and even did homage to them himself.

And Jehovah was angry with Solomon . . . and had commanded him concerning this thing, that he should not go after other gods: but he kept not that which Jehovah commanded. Wherefore Jehovah said unto Solomon, Forasmuch as this is done of thee . . . I will surely rend the kingdom from thee, and give it to thy servant. Notwithstanding in thy days I will not do it, for David thy father's sake, but I will rend it out of the hand of thy son (I Kings 11:9-12).

We are often warned by the inner monitor, the Spirit of truth, but we do not always heed the warning. Then difficulties began to appear. A revolt broke out in Edom, and Rezon, king of Syria, attacked Israel. The most formidable foe proved to be Jeroboam, an officer in Solomon's army. Jeroboam was told by the prophet Ahijah that Solomon's kingdom would be divided after his death, and that he (Jeroboam) would become king of the northern section of the land. When report of this prophecy reached Solomon, he tried to capture Jeroboam.

But Jeroboam escaped to Egypt, where he remained until the King's death.

Rehoboam, the son of Solomon, expected to follow his father on the throne and went to Shechem to receive allegiance from the northern tribes. In the meantime Jeroboam returned to Israel and acted as spokesman for the northern tribes who were intent on reform. He proposed:

Thy father made our yoke grievous: now therefore make thou the grievous service of thy father, and his heavy yoke which he put upon us, lighter, and we will serve thee (I King 12:4).

Rehoboam represents "that in man's consciousness which exalts the senses, that which is receptive to and comprehensive of the selfish demands of the sense thoughts and desires only" (M.D. 550). He first consulted the elder and experienced statesmen, who symbolize wisdom in handling affairs. They counseled him to grant the request and lessen the burdens placed upon the people. Then Rehoboam turned to his younger counselors, who were more impetuous and lacked good judgment. They advised a rule of even greater severity. When we are in the Rehoboam state of consciousness and exalt the senses, we do not follow the guidance of wisdom but choose the way of desire for power. Thus Rehoboam made answer:

My Father made your yoke heavy, but I will add to your yoke: my father chastised you with whips, but I will chastise you with scorpions (I Kings 12:14).

Decisions that are base and oppressive always result in a scattering of our forces. This is represented by a division of the kingdom. The ten northern tribes withdrew and established a kingdom that was called Israel, with Jeroboam as sovereign. Rehoboam retained Judah only.

The strong, well-protected country of David and Solomon was thus divided into two countries only slightly superior in power to those about them. Judah, the southern kingdom, was smaller and more conservative, due in large measure to its inland location and also to the fact that it had the city of Jerusalem and kept the dynasty of David. The northern kingdom, Israel, was several times larger and was more progressive, for through its territory ran the trade route between Assyria and Egypt, the largest and most important countries of that time. Nevertheless, Israel was so unstable in government and wandered so far from the religion of Jehovah that it lost its independence a century and a half before Judah was conquered.

Jeroboam represents the intellect functioning apart from Spirit. The intellect of itself cannot perceive the deep things of God, for they are "spiritually discerned" (I Cor. 2:14 A.V.) and only in spiritual consciousness can man truly worship God. In the Jeroboam state of mind we mistake shadow for substance and think that our spiritual obligation is discharged by our building sanctuaries. As the Temple was in Jerusalem, over which Rehoboam ruled, Jeroboam promptly set up shrines in Bethel and Dan, two cities in Israel, and "made two calves of gold" (I Kings 12:28) to represent Jehovah. He also sinned in selecting priests who were not of the sons of Levi. He allowed the shrines of Baal to remain, thus "provoking Jehovah to anger" (I Kings 14:15).

This symbolizes the substitution of false for true worship. The phrase used with respect to a king who followed Jeroboam that he "walked in the way of Jeroboam" (I Kings 16:2) means that when the intellect (Jeroboam) rules God is ignored and false deities are set up. The word Baal means "lord." Charles Fillmore comments:

It was the besetting sin of the ancient Hebrews to apply the name of the Lord to things formed instead of to the formless. All concepts of God as less than universal Mind are Baal. Whoever believes in a personal God tends toward a materialization of religion in all its aspects. When the mind is centered in the outer realm of consciousness, when the thoughts (people) are adverse to God, it retrogrades until that whole state of consciousness goes to pieces. This retrogression is by stages, from bad to worse (M.D. 494).

Judah, ruled by Rehoboam, was little better off. When we are controlled by sense consciousness (Rehoboam) or intellect (Jeroboam), unwholesome conditions quickly come into manifestation. There was war between the two Hebrew kingdoms, and Judah was attacked by Shishak, king of Egypt, and the Temple was plundered.

From the reign of Jeroboam until the time of Ahab, a period of about half a century, the northern kingdom, Israel, had a most unstable government. Five kings ruled, the only one of note being Omri, who ascended the throne in 887 B.C. Omri was a strong king from an outer point of view. He built the city of Samaria as a capital for Israel, gained control of Moab, made defensive alliances with Syria and Assyria, and was successful in diplomatic relations with Tyre.

Spiritually, Omri represents "an external movement of the mind in a whirl of discord, caused largely by a lack of spiritual development" (M.D. 493). What Omri did, therefore, was of temporary advantage only, and in marrying his son Ahab to the Tyrian princess Jezebel he set in motion a chain of events that were to have a disastrous effect upon Israel. Whatever entices us to move farther from God is detrimental and in the Omri state of consciousness; in this consciousness we are governed wholly by the outer appearance and unable to "judge righteous judgment" (John 7:24).

Because Judah did not swing so far from the Lord as did Israel, its outer conditions were better. Rehoboam was followed by his son Abijam, who ruled for only three years. Abijam represents a destructive phase of consciousness, for "he walked in all the sins of his father . . . and his heart was not perfect with Jehovah his God" (I Kings 15:3).

Asa, Abijam's son, was a good king and the first to bring about religious reforms since the division of the kingdom. He represents "the will working constructively" (M.D. 67). When man's will func-

tions in harmony with God the result is entirely
beneficial. Asa tried to rid his country of altars to
false Gods. He had faith in God when his country
was attacked by a vastly superior force of
Ethiopians:

> Asa cried unto Jehovah his God, and said, Jehovah,
> there is none besides thee to help, between the mighty
> and him that hath no strength: help us, O Jehovah our
> God; for we rely on thee, and in thy name are we come
> against this multitude (II Chron. 14:11).

When we rely on Him, we are always victorious
no matter how great the foe. This truth is brought
out repeatedly in Scripture. In giving our faith to the
Lord, we receive the assurance:

> Jehovah is with you, while ye are with him; and if ye
> seek him, he will be found of you; but if ye forsake him,
> he will forsake you. . . . But be ye strong, and let not your
> hands be slack; for your work shall be rewarded (II Chron.
> 15:2-7).

Would that we could sustain the faith we feel
when we have prayed and seen the manifestation of
spiritual power in the overcoming of some difficult
problem! But, because we have not yet reached a
steadfast consciousness of God's presence, we are
quite likely to forget Him when another trial comes.
This human tendency is outpictured in Asa. Baasha,
king of Israel, threatened Judah. And instead of
relying on the Lord, Asa sought an alliance with the
Syrians. For this he was rebuked by Hanani the
prophet·

Because thou hast relied on the king of Syria, and hast not relied on Jehovah thy God, therefore is the host of the king of Syria escaped out of thy hand. Were not the Ethiopians . . . a huge host, with chariots and horsemen exceeding many? yet, because thou didst rely on Jehovah, he delivered them into thy hand. For the eyes of Jehovah run to and fro throughout the whole earth, to show himself strong in the behalf of them whose heart is perfect toward him (II Chron. 16:7-9).

The prophets always represent a strong spiritual thought in consciousness that calls attention to our deficiencies and urges reliance on God. It is borne out throughout Scripture that when we trust ourselves and our affairs to Him, the outcome is good; when our dependence is on the outer, we fall short of complete victory. The prophet reminds us of this. Asa overcame the Ethiopians but by entering into a treaty with Syria to help him fight Israel, he increased his difficulties, for Syria later proved to be a more formidable enemy than Israel.

When one has started on the wrong path it is difficult not to continue on it. In the latter part of the King's life:

Asa was diseased in his feet . . . yet in his disease he sought not to Jehovah, but to the physicians. And Asa slept with his fathers, and died in the one and fortieth year of his reign (II Chron. 16:12, 13).

Nevertheless the total of Asa's life was on the side of the constructive. In none of the Bible characters, except Jesus, do we find the complete expression of the spiritual consciousness. The Old Testa-

ment records an evolving understanding of God on
the part of man, and in each person there is a mix-
ture of good and bad. When it is written of one of
the kings, he "did that which was right in the eyes
of Jehovah" (I Kings 15:11), it means that that king
expressed more of spiritual than nonspiritual qualities. When it is said of a ruler that, "he did that
which was evil in the sight of Jehovah" (I Kings
15:26), we know that destructive qualities pre-
dominated. The events reveal the action of both
states of mind. Not all the deeds of the "good kings"
were worthy, nor were all those of the "evil kings"
of a destructive nature. It is the general trend of a
life that must be considered.

An understanding of this is very helpful to us as
we journey toward the spiritual. We do not step into
the higher consciousness the moment there is the
intellectual comprehension that God is supreme.
Rather do we grow into it through many a rise and
fall. Asa and his son Jehoshaphat, who followed him
on the throne, were worthy kings, each trying to rid
his country (consciousness) of false gods (destructive thoughts). Each expressed strong spiritual
qualities, yet each made mistakes that had serious
consequences.

As we study the Bible, as we acquaint ourselves
with the many characters therein and view the events
that took place, we learn great lessons on how to
handle with divine wisdom situations in our own
lives. The enemies that attacked Israel symbolize
the erroneous states of mind that obsess us at times

and can be overcome only as we unify ourselves with the Lord indwelling. That the Hebrews were invariably victorious when they prayed, helps to stimulate our faith in prayer.

Jehoshaphat, like his father Asa, continued the religious reformation. He represents:

The development, in consciousness, of the divine idea of judgment. Jehovah, I AM, gives forth its idea of judgment, which is incorporated in man's consciousness and called Jehoshaphat. Communication with Jehovah is established when man, by dwelling in thought upon divine ideas, harmonizes his thought realm with Divine Mind (M.D. 331).

Jehoshaphat showed excellent judgment when his country was attacked by the Moabites and Ammonites, for he prayed:

O Jehovah, the God of our fathers, art not thou God in heaven? and art not thou ruler over all the kingdoms of the nations? and in thy hand is power and might, so that none is able to withstand thee. . . . we have no might against this great company that cometh against us; neither know we what to do: but our eyes are upon thee (II Chron. 20:6-12).

Such prayer brings the assurance:

Thus saith Jehovah unto you, Fear not ye, neither be dismayed by reason of this great multitude; for the battle is not yours, but God's. . . . Ye shall not need to fight in this *battle:* set yourselves, stand ye still, and see the salvation of Jehovah with you (II Chron. 20:15, 17).

We feel very joyful when it is revealed to us that the Lord is with us. Jehoshaphat said to his as-

sembled army, "Hear me, O Judah . . . believe in
Jehovah your God; so shall ye be established" (II
Chron. 20:20). Then he appointed singers to go
before the soldiers who were to sing songs of praise
and thanksgiving. "Give thanks unto Jehovah; for
his lovingkindness *endureth* for ever" (II Chron.
20:21). When we go at our task with gratitude to
the Lord in our hearts, we always triumph. The
battle is His, not ours. We have no strength apart
from the mighty One through whom we conquer.

Jehoshaphat temporarily healed the enmity between the kingdoms of Judah and Israel by allying
himself with Ahab, who had followed his father
Omri on the throne of Israel. However, Jehoshaphat
permitted himself to come under the influence of
Ahab, who symbolizes "Error states of consciousness based on false intellectual reasoning, or the intellect that has dropped to the level of sense worship" (M.D. 30).

The union of Jehoshaphat with Ahab represents
judgment warped by association with the intellect
that has been turned to sense desires. No good can
come of this. Ahab influenced Jehoshaphat to join
him in an attack upon Ramoth-Gilead. At first Jehoshaphat demurred and requested the counsel of
Micaiah, a true prophet of the Lord, who advised
against such an attack. Jehoshaphat did not heed.
(How many times we ask of God and then do not
heed!) The battle went against the Hebrew kings,
but when Jehoshaphat prayed, his life was spared.
Then the prophet Jehu said to him:

Shouldest thou help the wicked, and love them that hate Jehovah? for this thing wrath is upon thee from before Jehovah. Nevertheless there are good things found in thee, in that thou hast put away the Asheroth out of the land, and hast set thy heart to seek God (II Chron. 19:2, 3).

With Jehoshaphat, as with Asa, we find righteousness as well as wrongdoing. We always demonstrate, however, in accordance with the predominant thought in consciousness, and when we are like Jehoshaphat and use good judgment the greater part of the time, our work is mainly beneficial to ourselves and others.

CHAPTER XI

Elijah and Elisha

I Kings 17-22; II Kings 1-14:22;
II Chronicles 21-25

T
HE REIGN OF Ahab in Israel (875-854 B.C.) marked a period of material prosperity but religious decline. It is important in our spiritual study of the Bible because it brought forth two of the greatest of the Hebrew men of God, Elijah and Elisha.

Ahab had married Jezebel, daughter of Ethbaal, king of Tyre, and she exerted a great influence over Ahab and Israel. Jezebel brought to Israel from her native country the practice of Baal worship and used all her power to compel the Hebrews to desert Jehovah and worship the special Baal called Melkart. If Jezebel had been content with a temple to this Baal for her own use (such an arrangement was often allowed foreign princesses), probably no great harm would have been done. But she had temples erected in Samaria and elsewhere in Israel, formed a large priesthood, and made a determined effort to kill out the worship of Jehovah. Jezebel represents:

The animal soul, unbridled passions of sense consciousness. When the union of the ruling identity in the intellect (King Ahab) and the licentious desires of the body is complete, the whole man is involved in error. This is rearing "an altar for Baal in the house of Baal." Jezebel could also be called the ruling emotions on the physical plane of consciousness (M.D. 352).

It was evident that something had to be done to save the worship of Jehovah. There was a man for the job, and his name was Elijah. Elijah represents "the spiritual I AM of man's consciousness" (M.D. 191). Were it not for the Elijah self within us, our consciousness would be completely infiltrated with sense desires (Jezebel), for there are times when Jezebel rises with great power. Then Elijah, the spiritual self, comes forth to combat these destructive phases of mind. In each individual there is conflict between Elijah and Jezebel, and this conflict is dramatically depicted in the Bible narrative.

Elijah, called the Tishbite, was a native of Gilead, a holy man, and an ascetic. When word was brought to him that the religion of Jehovah was threatened by Jezebel he left his desert home and took matters in charge. Promptly predicting a three-year drought as a judgment and warning to the Israelites, Elijah retired to the brook Cherith. "And the ravens brought him bread and flesh in the morning, and bread and flesh in the evening; and he drank of the brook" (I Kings 17:6). The one who champions the spiritual cause is always divinely provided for.

Whenever we are under the guidance of the I AM, we can use spiritual power in performing mighty works, such as Elijah did when he increased the meal and oil for the woman of Zarepath and raised the widow's son.

Finally it was time for a contest between Jehovah and Baal. Elijah summoned a great assembly

at Mount Carmel and challenged the prophets of
Baal to call upon their god to consume the sacrifice
that had been prepared. But, though they cried to
Baal from morning until noon, "there was no voice,
nor any that answered" (I Kings 18:26). Then
Elijah built an altar of twelve stones in the name of
Jehovah and made a trench about it, which was filled
with water.

And it came to pass at the time of the offering of
the *evening* oblation, that Elijah the prophet came near,
and said, O Jehovah, the God of Abraham, of Isaac,
and of Israel, let it be known this day that thou art God
in Israel . . . that this people may know that thou, Jehovah, art God, and *that* thou hast turned their heart back
again. Then the fire of Jehovah fell, and consumed the
burnt-offering, and the wood, and the stones, and the
dust, and licked up the water that was in the trench. And
when all the people saw it, they fell on their faces: and
they said, Jehovah, he is God (I Kings 18:36-39).

This is one of the most spectacular miracles
recorded in Scripture, and we cannot read it without feeling exalted at the power of God evidenced
through one who put his entire faith in Him. Today
we do not have conditions similar to those of Elijah's
day, and no one calls upon God to consume a sacrifice, but we do have human conditions that seem as
difficult of solution as that which confronted the
prophet of the Lord. The many prophets of Baal
who opposed Elijah represent the multitude of adverse thoughts opposing the one phase of consciousness that would hold to Truth. This miracle is the
fulfillment of the promise, "One man of you shall

chase a thousand; for Jehovah your God, he it is that fighteth for you" (Josh. 23:10).

Elijah knew that if the people would turn to Jehovah the drought would end. Though there was not a cloud in the sky, Elijah said to Ahab, "Get thee up, eat and drink; for there is the sound of abundance of rain" (I Kings 18:41). Then Elijah went to the top of Mount Carmel to pray. Six times he sent his servant to look toward the sea, and each time the servant returned to his master, saying, "There is nothing."

"And it came to pass at the seventh time, that he said, Behold, there ariseth a cloud out of the sea, as small as a man's hand" (I Kings 18:44).

That was enough for Elijah. He knew a downpour was on its way.

Can we have such a sense of surety regarding the successful outworking of a problem when there is even a slight evidence of the answer to prayer? When we receive a wonderful evidence of the power of God, we feel that we shall never doubt again. That is what Elijah thought but he reckoned without Jezebel. Elijah, in what he perhaps termed "righteous indignation," had caused 450 prophets of Baal to be slain, and Jezebel swore vengeance against him. He fled to Beersheba, discouraged and disheartened, and throwing himself down under a juniper tree, prayed to die. "It is enough; now, O Jehovah, take away my life" (I Kings 19:4).

Elijah was feeling very sorry for himself, as we sometimes do when things go awry after we have

tried hard to live in accordance with our spiritual
ideal. There is the feeling, at least momentarily,
that the Lord has deserted us, and it is such a sick-
ening sensation that we think all is lost and there
is no use in going on. However, Elijah's prayer was
one of complete surrender to God, and he dropped
off to sleep. He knew there was nothing more he
could do about the situation, and in his withdrawal
from it, the Lord took over. In the Biblical account
we are told that an angel touched him, told him to
arise and eat and there was a cake and a cruse of
water before him.

Charles Fillmore states that an angel, metaphysically considered, "is the projection into consciousness of a spiritual idea direct from the foun-
tainhead, Jehovah" (M.D. 52). In other words,
Elijah received the illumination that there was still
something he should do, and he journeyed "forty
days and forty nights unto Horeb the mount of God"
(I Kings 19:8). There he received the profound revelation that God is not in the wind, nor in the earth-
quake, nor in the fire, but in a "still small voice" (I
Kings 19:12).

Three commands were given Elijah: he was to
anoint Hazael king over Syria, Jehu king over Israel,
and anoint Elisha to be a prophet in his (Elijah's)
stead. The third command, to anoint Elisha, was the
first to be obeyed. Both Elijah and Elisha represent
the I AM in activity, but Elijah symbolizes the
strength and firmness of spiritual power, whereas
Elisha, a type of Christ, represents the compassionate

love and devotion of Spirit. Functioning together, they express the marvelous power of God for good.

Man is always tested when he puts his foot on the spiritual path. The first test comes when we hear the call to follow. In the case of many of our Bible characters they responded immediately, leaving whatever they were doing. Such were Moses, Elisha, other prophets, and the apostles of Jesus. Elisha was plowing when Elijah came and threw his mantle over him. Promptly Elisha made a sacrifice to the Lord, "and went after Elijah, and ministered unto him" (I Kings 19:21).

Apparently Elijah and his disciple Elisha worked together for some time. Then Elijah's work was done, and he knew it.

And Elijah said unto Elisha, Tarry here, I pray thee; for Jehovah hath sent me as far as Bethel. And Elisha said, As Jehovah liveth, and as thy soul liveth, I will not leave thee (II Kings 2:2).

There are times when we must be very persistent in holding fast to the spiritual. Remember Jacob's refusal to release the angel of the Lord. Three times Elijah urged Elisha to remain where he was. Also the members of the prophetic guild of the cities through which they passed reminded Elisha that Elijah was to leave him. Still the faithful Elisha went on with his master. After leaving Jericho Elijah parted the waters of the Jordan, and the two passed over dry land.

By his persistence in holding to the spiritual

(Elijah), Elisha earned the right to accept the blessing of his master. Elijah said to him:

Ask what I shall do for thee, before I am taken from thee. And Elisha said, I pray thee, let a double portion of thy spirit be upon me. And he said, Thou hast asked a hard thing: nevertheless, if thou see me when I am taken from thee, it shall be so unto thee; but if not, it shall not be so (II Kings 2:9, 10).

Elisha asked a spiritual boon. Is that our desire or is it merely that God will give us a specific blessing, such as health or prosperity or the outworking of a tedious problem? Charles Fillmore states in the *Metaphysical Dictionary:*

The double portion of Elijah's spirit for which Elisha asked is the positive and negative, or "yes" and "no," of Truth. Elisha, the tender, retiring one, needs the ability to say yes and no with all the positiveness of Elijah. He can have this only by perceiving the true character of the change that is taking place in consciousness. Elijah is not taken away but is translated to a more interior plane. There is opened to the one who goes through this change a conscious unity with spiritual energies of which he has been heretofore ignorant. The chariot and horses represent the vehicles and vital forces that attend the transformation (M.D. 193).

Elisha did see the translation of Elijah, and "he took up also the mantle of Elijah that fell from him, and went back, and stood by the bank of the Jordan" (II Kings 2:13). There was work to be done, and with Elijah's mantle, symbolic of a double portion of the great prophet's spirit that Elisha had received, Elisha was fully equipped.

Elisha is often referred to by Bible commentators as a forerunner of Jesus. His character and his marvelous works are easily recognized as proceeding from the same spirit that inspired Jesus, and his gentleness and simplicity are paralleled only in the Master. It is not difficult to see in Elisha an incarnation of the Christ, and he was in a certain degree God manifest. Jesus was a fuller manifestation of the same spirit (M.D. 193).

Many and wonderful were the miracles performed by Elisha. Perhaps the best known are: increase of the widow's oil—II Kings 4; raising the son of the Shunammite woman—II Kings 4; miraculous feeding of a hundred men—II Kings 4; healing of Naaman—II Kings 5; and kindly treatment of the Syrians—II Kings 6.

The ministry of Elijah and Elisha extended over a period in which many changes took place in the Hebrew kingdoms of Israel and Judah. While both the prophets were natives of Israel, the affairs of Israel and Judah were so intertwined that the influence of Elijah and Elisha extended to Judah also. In viewing this period from the standpoint of spiritual interpretation, the sovereigns of Israel and Judah represent the rule of error states of consciousness that were minimized and often overcome by the strong spiritual qualities represented by the prophets of the Lord. When any one of the attributes of the I AM comes to the fore in consciousness, the destructive qualities of the sense mind are overthrown and order and harmony are for a time restored.

Elisha fulfilled Jehovah's command to Elijah that Jehu be anointed king of Israel. Jehu signifies "the monitor or inner guide that intuitively perceives the right" (M.D. 334). Jehu brought about a revolution that deposed of Jehoram, the reigning king of the house of Ahab, and destroyed Jezebel. While the revolution was violent (as we sometimes are when in the Jehu consciousness we perceive the right but are overzealous in destroying evil), it did serve to cleanse Tyrian Baalism from the land.

The influence of Jezebel and Baalism had been felt in Judah also, for Athaliah, the daughter of Ahab and Jezebel, had married Jehoram, the son of Jehoshaphat, king of Judah. During the reigns of Jehoram and his son Ahaziah, Athaliah was a strong influence. After the death of Ahaziah, Athaliah had all the members of the royal house slain, with the exception of the child Joash, who had been secretly spirited away and was kept in hiding by the priest Jehoiada for six years, during which time Athaliah reigned.

Athaliah represents:

The feminine or love nature in man wholly given to selfishness. Its dominant ambition is to rule, and it destroys everything that stands in the way of its attaining this ambition (M.D. 77).

Such a state of consciousness is often mighty but its defeat is assured even from the beginning of its rule. Man is a spiritual being, and spiritual forces are always at work within him. He may be dominated again and again by the sense consciousness in its various phases (represented by the reign of Athaliah), but the time comes when the spiritual self reasserts itself. This is illustrated in the Bible by the revolt instigated by Jehoiada. Jehoiada signifies: "the divine law of justice, which brings to retribution all who transgress its law. He calls into action the forces that destroy error" (M.D. 330).

As a result of the revolution Athaliah was slain. The rightful ruler, the boy Joash, was placed upon the throne. Thus the Davidic line was continued. Joash represents the will. As long as Jehoiada lived to guide him, Joash was a good king, but after the priest's death Joash degenerated and became domineering and vindictive. "This shows the necessity of the will's being guided by the inner Spirit of wisdom and justice" (M.D. 330).

The ministry of Elisha continued during much of this period. We read of his advising a number of the kings and predicting the result of righteous and unrighteous conduct. Finally his great work was complete:

And Elisha died, and they buried him. Now the bands of the Moabites invaded the land at the coming in of the year. And it came to pass, as they were burying a man, that, behold, they spied a band; and they cast the man into the sepulchre of Elisha; and as soon as the man touched the bones of Elisha, he revived, and stood up on his feet (II Kings 13:20, 21).

The Spirit of the Lord within man never dies and when one has been loyal to this Spirit, his influence reanimates all who contact him. The bones of Elisha stand for the tangible presence of the great prophet. Today, as we read of his wonderful words, of the stanchness of his mind, of the gentleness of his heart, we "touch" him and something of the Spirit of God, which radiated so powerfully through him, vitalizes and restores the self of us that is seemingly dead, perhaps in fear or discouragement.

The life and teachings of these two great champions of God, Elijah and Elisha, put another layer on the foundation of spiritual consciousness that had been slowly built by the Israelites. The superstructure was soon to be erected by that remarkable group of men known as the "literary prophets."

CHAPTER XII

Eighth Century Prophets of Israel

JEROBOAM II became king of Israel in 783 B.C. and reigned for forty years. This was a time of material prosperity, peace, and extension of territory. Much of the land east of the Jordan that had been taken by Syria in previous years was again restored to Israel.

The reason for unusual quiet was due to the fact that Syria, which had warred with Israel for generations, was engaged in struggles with Assyria. Assyria, the great country to the north, had been slowly rising in power since the early part of the ninth century B.C. Her first outstanding king, Ashurbanipal, founded a mighty empire. He also displayed savagery and ruthlessness in conquest that made the Assyrians feared by all the neighboring lands. The policy of Assyria was to gain control of all of Palestine in preparation for the conquest of Egypt. To carry out this program, Assyria had to conquer Syria first. Therefore, during the reign of Jeroboam II, Israel was left in peace.

The prophets of this era perceived Assyria's plan, and foresaw that the Hebrew countries were in grave danger. Neither Israel nor Judah was strong enough to resist Assyria by force of arms. Their only strength was in the Lord, and the life they were living was such as to separate them from Him. This

145

the prophets pointed out, but the people would not listen. They were reveling in the good times of the moment and did not want to be told that their conduct was unbecoming to a nation dedicated to the service of Jehovah. The upper and influential classes were highly satisfied with their ruler and their God. Jeroboam was an able king, and the sanctuaries of Israel, especially Bethel, Gilgal, and Samaria, were filled with worshipers offering sacrifices to the Lord, who prospered them.

From a spiritual viewpoint there was much to be desired. Material prosperity is liable to bring great social evils in its train, and so it did in Israel. The prophetic writers of II Kings said of Jeroboam II that he did "evil in the sight of Jehovah" (II Kings 3:2).

Once again the Lord raised up leaders to speak in His name to the Children of Israel. Throughout their history the Hebrews had had prophets, but beginning with the eighth century B.C., there came to them one of the most remarkable groups of men the world has ever known. They are referred to as "literary prophets" because they wrote their sermons, or had them written. These prophets were not soothsayers, and their purpose was not to predict the future by some occult power, as did the false prophets. Their aim was to give God's message to the people of their day and to say wherein a violation of the divine will would bring dire results. "Thus saith Jehovah" (Amos 5:4) is the prophetic refrain.

All the prophets labored zealously in an effort

to turn the people from idolatry to the worship of the true God. While not one of them succeeded during his lifetime, except temporarily, the great spiritual messages each gave preserved the religion of Israel, purified it to a large extent, and paved the way for the coming of Christianity. Each prophet did his own work in his own way and, though the latter prophets were undoubtedly influenced by those who preceded them, each was an isolated individual with tremendous courage born of the conviction that he was the mouthpiece of God.

The eighth century produced four prophets, Amos and Hosea in Israel, and I Isaiah and Micah in Judah. They were fully aware of the unwholesome conditions that prevailed and were certain that the Hebrew countries were doomed unless there was a rapid and radical change. Earthly power was in the hands of the Assyrians, but spiritual power, always superior, could be with the Hebrews if they would heed the word of the Lord and put themselves under His protection.

Regardless of how superb we acknowledge the messages of the prophets to be from a religious or literary standpoint, we do not get the full benefit of them unless we perceive these prophets as our teachers for today. Historically they belong to an age long past; metaphysically they represent different phases of the Spirit of truth indwelling, each having some word that is indispensable. On occasions we need to comprehend God as the principle underlying existence itself; then we listen to what Amos has to say. At other times we yearn for a deeper feeling of the compassion and never-ending love of our heavenly Father; then we listen to Hosea.

At the time the prophets began their work both Hebrew countries were definitely "off the beam" in a spiritual sense. This period is similar to the state of mind into which we sometimes lapse where material interests gain precedence over spiritual ones. Such consciousness is always the forerunner of destructive outer conditions. Why not change it? The messages of the prophets tell us how. We can see ourselves in the people of their day and we want to guard against thinking and doing those very things that are bound to terminate in a loss of good.

No matter how far we wander from a spiritual standard, the Bible assures us that there is always a way open to God. The prophets reveal milestones along that way.

Amos 750 B.C.

The Book of Amos is the earliest complete portion of the Bible that we may read today just as it was written more than seven centuries before the beginning of the Christian Era. Portions of the Pentateuch and the historical books had been written much earlier but they did not reach their final form until long after the days of Amos.

Amos was a native of Tekoa, a small town near Jerusalem. He was a herdsman and a dresser of sycamore trees. To dispose of his wool he often went to the cities of Israel that afforded a good market.

There he saw many evidences of the moral corruption of the people. The upper classes were rich and powerful. They imposed exorbitant taxes on the poor and cheated them in land and food. Bribery was rampant in the courts, immorality was condoned, and there was a total disregard for the commandments of the Lord. The sins of the people were those of any person to whom the things of the world mean more than the things of God.

Amos represents "conscience, which shepherds the natural forces of mind and body. . . . Amos in us warns us when we have trangressed the divine law" (M.D. 48). Let us think of Amos as the higher phase of our being, revealing Truth to us. The fundamental lesson he teaches is that God is the great law governing life in its entirety. His righteous will is supreme and the one who violates it breaks only himself. When we are like the Israelites and indulge in practices that are in direct opposition to God's law, we reap as tragic a harvest as did those people of ancient days. Amos gave his message in the hope that the people might better understand the Lord and change their ways. It is ever the function of conscience to show wherein we are falling short and draw us closer to the spiritual.

Suddenly appearing at the sanctuary in Bethel on a feast day, Amos gave his first sermon. He declared that Israel and Judah, as well as all the surrounding nations, were laden with iniquity and that great hardships would result. Amos introduced an entirely new idea of the Lord in this initial message.

Prior to this time the Hebrews had considered Jehovah as solely their God and thought He had no connection with other nations. They believed each nation had its own god, even as Jehovah was theirs, and the fact that Assyria was having great success led some to wonder whether the Assyrian gods were not more powerful than Jehovah. Amos insisted that Jehovah was the only God and that He ruled over other nations as fully as over Israel and Judah. Natural and political calamities were also traceable to violations of His will.

Amos conceded that Jehovah's relation to the Hebrews was a special one. This was a privilege but it also entailed a responsibility, and the chosen people would pay a heavier penalty for their sins. Thus saith the Lord, "You only have I known of all the families of the earth: therefore I will visit upon you all your iniquities" (Amos 3:2).

We accept one God, supreme and all-powerful, but we do not always realize that the closer our individual relation to Him is, the greater our moral and spiritual obligations are. For example, anyone who steals, whether or not he thinks himself justified, breaks a commandment of God and must pay a penalty, but the one who has been spiritually quickened and yet yields to temptation gets a worse result. One's having been privileged to know God, even to some degree, aggravates the transgression. Amos knew that any nation disobedient to the principle of rightness would reap an ill effect, and said this by predicting misfortunes for neighboring countries.

He reminded the Israelites, however, that their punishment would be more severe.

At the sanctuaries the most elaborate ceremonials were conducted. Amos insisted that God wanted righteousness:

> I hate, I despise your feasts, and I will take no delight in your solemn assemblies. Yea, though ye offer me your burnt-offerings and meal-offerings, I will not accept them; neither will I regard the peace-offerings of your fat beasts. . . . But let justice roll down as waters, and righteousness as a mighty stream (Amos 5:21, 24).

The outer forms of religion, such as attending church, contributing to its support, supporting worthy charitable organizations, are meaningless unless we sustain them by spiritual thought and conduct. It is much more important for us to be just in dealing with our fellow men. Amos had every respect for the observance of feast days, as they were part of the religious custom of the age, but he pointed out that good deeds without a good spirit are not pleasing to the Lord.

Because the Israelites had lost the true spirit of religion, irreverence was another sin of which they were guilty. To the merchants the Sabbath was an irritating interruption in their commercial life. The feasts, which were supposed to be in praise of Jehovah, had become simply orgies where men and women drank to excess and indulged in the most immoral practices. While Israel seemed to be great and mighty the prophet insisted that such sins had made her so weak spiritually that the day would

come when she would need the Lord but would be
unable to find Him. He predicted a famine, "not a
famine of bread, nor a thirst for water, but of hearing the words of Jehovah" (Amos 8:11). Her transgressions had alienated Israel from God, and she
was without His protection:

> Thus saith the Lord Jehovah: An adversary *there shall
> be,* even round about the land; and he shall bring down
> thy strength from thee, and thy palaces shall be plundered
> (Amos 3:11).

To bring out the lesson that each individual, as
well as each nation, is measured by the law of God,
Amos told the parable of the plumb line:

> Thus he showed me: and, behold, the Lord stood be-
> side a wall made by a plumb-line, with a plumb-line in his
> hand. And Jehovah said unto me, Amos, what seest thou?
> And I said, A plumb-line. Then said the Lord, Behold, I
> will set a plumb-line in the midst of my people Israel; I
> will not again pass by them any more; and the high places
> of Isaac shall be desolate, and the sanctuaries of Israel
> shall be laid waste; and I will rise against the house of
> Jeroboam with the sword (Amos 7:7-9).

When we deviate from God's law our lives get
out of plumb or balance. This is apparent when
judged by the divine standard (plumb line) to which
we are frequently exposed by the Lord or the law.
Our Maker gives us every opportunity to know
righteousness and live in accord therewith, but if
we turn from Him the day comes when sentence is
passed. "I will rise against the house of Jeroboam
with the sword."

But there is also mercy in the heart of the Almighty for the one who seeks the higher way. Thus Amos counseled:

Hate the evil, and love the good, and establish justice in the gate: it may be that Jehovah, the God of hosts, will be gracious unto the remnant of Joseph (Amos 5:15).

Amos was a stern prophet. To him God was the absolute power in the universe and His law could not be broken with impunity. Israel had sinned and was sinning daily, but if she would turn to God and repent, she could be saved.

Few people like to have their shortcomings paraded before them, and the citizens of Israel were no exception. The prophet was abused and turned out of the sanctuary for being a troublemaker and disloyal to king and country. But his messages have lived because they are Truth. Though crushed to earth for a time, they rise in the words of later prophets and provide a sure guidance for us.

Hosea (745-735 B.C.)

Hardly had the voice of Amos rung through the land to the consternation of some and the indifference of others, before another prophet also declared the word of the Lord fearlessly. His name was Hosea, and in temperament he was almost the opposite of Amos. Hosea conceived God, not as the great law of the cosmos, but as Israel's Father who loved His erring children in spite of their sins. This prophet was likewise aware of the national corruption and denounced it unsparingly. Even in his denunciation, however, he was gentler and more sympathetic than Amos. He sought to give his people such insight into the nature of God, whom he knew to be a God of love, that they could not worship false deities nor trangress His commandments.

Charles Fillmore states that Hosea represents the "I AM identity" (M.D. 286), the spiritual self of us that knows all men are sons of the Most High, all are recipients of the divine love that is constantly being poured in and through us. How can we, being the objects of His devotion, turn from Him?

The prophet's own personal life furnishes a good example of Jehovah's relation to His children: He had married a woman named Gomer who was a temple prostitute, and loved her deeply even though he knew of her unfaithfulness. To Hosea this exemplified God's love for Israel, a love that had served them and, even in spite of their iniquities, could not desert them. Thus said the Lord:

> When Israel was a child, then I loved him, and called my son out of Egypt. . . . they sacrificed unto the Baalim, and burned incense to graven images. Yet I taught Ephraim to walk; I took them on my arms; but they know not that I healed them. I drew them with cords of a man, with bands of love; and I was to them as they that lift up the yoke on their jaws . . . How shall I give thee up, Ephraim? how shall I cast thee off, Israel? . . . my heart is turned within me, my compassions are kindled together. I will not execute the fierceness of mine anger, I will not return to destroy Ephraim: for I am God . . . the Holy One in the midst of thee (Hos. 11:1-4, 8, 9).

As we realize something of the compassion of our

Father for His creatures, a great sense of humility sweeps over us, and there comes the urging from this Hosea self (the I AM) to seek union with Him:

> O Israel, return unto Jehovah thy God; for thou hast fallen by thine iniquity. Take with you words, and return unto Jehovah: say unto him, Take away all iniquity, and accept that which is good: so will we render *as* bullocks *the offering of* our lips (Hos. 14:1, 2).

When we return to our Father in prayer, His forgiveness is always forthcoming, and we, too, hear His promise given through the lips of this great prophet:

> I will heal their backsliding, I will love them freely . . . I will be as the dew unto Israel; he shall blossom as the lily, and cast forth his roots as Lebanon. His branches shall spread, and his beauty shall be as the olive-tree . . . They that dwell under his shadow shall return; they shall revive *as* the grain, and blossom as the vine (Hos. 14:4-7).

The prophets Amos and Hosea knew all too well what the result of Israel's sins would be and tried to stem the waves of disaster by counseling repentance and return to God, but the stern rebukes of Amos and the pleadings of Hosea fell on deaf ears. Israel was at peace and rich, and the people saw no reason to change their ways. This attitude is symbolic of the consciousness that is closed to spiritual guidance because it feels neither desire nor need for the Lord. But external good cannot be sustained without a good or spiritual consciousness, and the divine judgment must come to fruition. The events of the next two decades brought about the destruction of Israel.

Hosea began his prophetic career during the last years of the reign of Jeroboam II. The prosperity and power of that period terminated with Jeroboam's death (743 B.C.). For the next twenty-one years disastrous changes took place with amazing rapidity. Zachariah, the son of Jeroboam, ruled for six months and was slain. This inaugurated a political war, and the next several years marked one of continuous strife. Tiglath-pileser IV had become king of Assyria, and knowing the weakened condition of Israel, he marched south and invaded the land. Menahem, the then reigning king, was not able to offer effective resistance and kept his throne only by paying an enormous tribute.

This gave rise to great dissatisfaction in Israel, and Pekah, who had taken the throne by force, tried to throw off the Assyrian yoke. He allied himself with Rezin, king of Syria, and asked Judah to join them in fighting Assyria. Ahaz, king of Judah, refused and was attacked by Pekah and Rezin. Thoroughly terrified, Ahaz called on Tiglath-pileser for assistance, which was rendered promptly. The Assyrians came storming down on Israel, took some of her territory and carried hundreds of Israelites into captivity. Syria, the other rebel, was utterly crushed. Judah was spared but only at the price of vassalage. (The effect of this upon Judah will be discussed in the next chapter.)

In Israel there was an immediate uprising against Pekah. He was overthrown, and Hoshea was seated on the throne. He agreed to pay Assyria a yearly tribute, and there was peace for a short time. As soon as Tiglath-pileser died, Hoshea decided to revolt and was supported by Egypt. Forthwith the new king of Assyria, Shalmanezer IV, swept down on Israel, captured Hoshea, and laid siege to Samaria. The city was able to hold out for three years, during which time Shalmanezer died and his son Sargon II became king. Finally, late in the year 722 B.C., Samaria fell and the kingdom of Israel came to an end.

The best element of the defeated population was deported to Northern Mesopotamia and Media. Foreign colonists were brought in and they, along with the humbler Israelites, were under the complete domination of Assyria. Some of the deported Israelites might have made their way back home in later years, but the majority were absorbed by the peoples among whom they were settled. Thus the ten tribes were effectively lost. Though there have been many theories regarding them, history gives the verdict that they maintained neither their national nor religious identity. The Bible has this to say of them:

And the children of Israel walked in all the sins of Jeroboam which he did; they departed not from them; until Jehovah removed Israel out of his sight, as he spake by all his servants the prophets. So Israel was carried away out of their own land to Assyria unto this day (II Kings 17:22, 23).

From a spiritual viewpoint the entire period represents a time when the individual is overwhelmed by trials. By refusing to listen to the word of the

Lord we function in human consciousness only and
sow seeds of iniquity, the harvest of which is
calamity. The things we believe to be stable and
sure are swept away, and it seems that all is lost.
But because we are creatures of God and have within
us His life, there is the continuation of existence.
The Children of Israel, though reduced to the kingdom of Judah, live on. There is always a spiritual
part of us, a residue, a remnant that will, in time,
learn its lessons and find its way to God. The ongoing of man is pictured in the history of the
southern kingdom, Judah.

CHAPTER XIII

Eighth Century Prophets of Judah

II Kings 15-20; II Chronicles 28-32;
Isaiah 1-39; Micah

UZZIAH, THE GRANDSON of Joash, became king of Judah in 779 B.C., about four years after Jeroboam II began his reign in Israel. Uzziah ruled for approximately forty years and in many respects the conditions in Judah were similar to those in Israel during the same period. While we are told in II Kings 15:3 that Uzziah "did that which was right in the eyes of Jehovah," and his country prospered, nevertheless he permitted the high places (sanctuaries of Baal) to remain. Tyrian Baalism, introduced by Jezebel in the preceding century, had been driven out of Israel and Judah, but the native religion of Baal, which had been in Canaan since the Hebrews first entered the land under Joshua, still flourished, and Uzziah permitted it.

The name Uzziah means "Jehovah is strength" (M.D. 671), and he was a strong king in many respects. His strength, however, belonged to the realm of the physical and mental. When man's attention is confined to material success alone, he is not apt to be obedient to the Lord, and then there is the breaking up of some phase of his nature. "Jehovah smote the king, so that he was a leper unto the day of his death" (II Kings 15:5).

The Bible frequently records that Jehovah

brought disaster to a person because of his transgressions. We should remember that one aspect of God is principle or law, and when we deviate from His law, limitation is the result. The Hebrews believed that righteousness insured blessings even as sin brought suffering, so when a man was afflicted in any way or the nation lost a battle, the prophet historians simply said that Jehovah was responsible. We can get much closer to the real meaning of such expressions when we understand that God is the natural law operating in the lives of men. It is not God as a sort of superman who is angry or condemnatory, or who punishes mankind; rather God is principle and as such gives back to all in exact proportion to their giving. In the wrong act itself is the seed of the penalty.

Much the same political, social, moral, and religious evils existed in Judah as existed in Israel, during Uzziah's reign, and the masses had no realization of how far short they had fallen from the ideals preached by the great spiritual teachers of their race. The times demanded a man of vast spiritual insight and the courage to drive his message home. Such a man was I Isaiah, who began his ministry in Judah while Hosea was still speaking in Israel.

The Book of Isaiah is really a fine piece of literature. At least three prophets were responsible for it, and perhaps more. Chapters 1 through 39 are, in the main, the messages of I Isaiah, the statesman prophet, whose ministry began during the reign of Uzziah, about 740 B.C. The second portion of the book, chapters 40 through 55, contains the work of the great unknown prophet, referred to as II Isaiah or Deutero-Isaiah, who preached to the Jews during the latter part of the Exile. Chapters 56 through 66 were written after the Jews returned from Babylonia, and the author is known as III Isaiah or Trito-Isaiah. The messages of these three men mark the highest point of Hebrew prophecy.

I Isaiah (740-695 B.C.)

Unlike Amos, Hosea, and his later contemporary Micah, who were men of the country and had no familiarity with court circles, I Isaiah lived in Jerusalem and belonged to the aristocratic class. He may have been a member of the royal family. His career lasted about forty-five years. (For convenience we shall refer to I Isaiah simply as Isaiah throughout this chapter.)

While Isaiah was a young man he had a vision of Jehovah upon His throne, majestic and holy, and in the vision the prophet received his call to the Lord's service:

Then said I, Woe is me! for I am undone; because I am a man of unclean lips, and I dwell in the midst of a people of unclean lips: for mine eyes have seen the King, Jehovah of hosts.

Then flew one of the seraphim unto me, having a live coal in his hand . . . and he touched my mouth with it, and said, Lo, this hath touched thy lips; and thine iniquity is taken away, and thy sin forgiven. And I heard the voice of the Lord, saying, Whom shall I send, and who will go for us? Then I said, Here am I; send me (Isa. 6:5-8).

Our first spiritual quickening brings a feeling of personal unworthiness intermingled with a tremendous reverence for the Holy One, the sublime Presence, the great spiritual reality. It also brings a response, "Here am I; send me."

Isaiah represents "the higher self, that in us which discerns the reality, the real character of spiritual man, and fearlessly proclaims it; spiritual understanding" (M.D. 300). When the spiritual consciousness, symbolized by Isaiah, is quickened in us, we perceive God's righteous will, declare it, and obey it ourselves. We do not fluctuate in our allegiance to the spiritual but remain steadfast through trying conditions. The prophet Isaiah exemplified this consciousness throughout the years of his ministry.

Jotham, the son of Uzziah, had ruled in his father's stead during the period of the king's illness, and ascended the throne about 740 B.C. He was followed a few years later by Ahaz. Ahaz began his reign as a young man and proved to be a most unwise sovereign. When threatened by Pekah of Israel and Rezin of Damascus, who sought to form a coalition of Palestine states against Assyria, Ahaz chose an alliance with Assyria instead. Isaiah was bitterly opposed to this action. He advised the king to trust solely in Jehovah and to avoid all entangling treaties. Ahaz turned a deaf ear to the prophet, paid homage to the Assyrian king in person and aped his customs, having an altar built in Jerusalem like that of the Assyrians. Thus when Israel and Damascus were defeated in 732 B.C. and Samaria was destroyed ten years later, Judah was spared, though she was forced to pay an enormous tribute yearly to Assyria.

The destruction of Israel in 722 B.C. was a warning to Judah, and for a time the little kingdom accepted Assyrian domination without protest. In 715 B.C. Ahaz died and Hezekiah came to the throne. He was a noble prince and one of the few righteous kings Judah had had since Solomon's day. It is highly probable that Hezekiah had been under Isaiah's influence during his boyhood, since the life of the King in later years definitely showed the effects of Isaiah's ideas.

Spiritually, Hezekiah represents "the expression of the spiritual strength in the executive power of the mind" (M.D. 277). It was inevitable, therefore, that under Hezekiah a wave of reform swept through Judah. The Temple, which had been defiled by idol worshipers during the reign of Ahaz, was cleansed and renovated, and the Passover was again observed. The reformation went even farther, and many social abuses were corrected:

And in every work that he [Hezekiah] began in the service of the house of God, and in the law, and in the commandments, to seek his God, he did it with all his heart, and prospered (II Chron. 31:21).

When the Hezekiah faculty of mind (spiritual strength) comes to the fore, we become active immediately in correcting wrong conditions. The consciousness is cleansed of many of its errors, and we establish regular periods of prayer. This leads to the correction of outer ills, for when the Temple (spiritual consciousness) is purified salutary effects result in our lives. As we put our hearts into this good work, we always prosper.

Throughout this period the little country of Judah was in a precarious position. The people resented the yearly tribute that had to be paid to Assyria, and king and statesmen were constantly urged by Egypt to rebel against Assyria. Egypt wanted the whole of Palestine as a buffer state between her and the mighty Assyrians. In 705 B.C. Sargon II was assassinated, and it looked as if the Assyrian empire would crumble. Egypt promptly urged Hezekiah to ally Judah with her, and some of the finest messages of Isaiah were delivered in the vain attempt to prevent such a coalition. Isaiah insisted that Egypt promised much but would perform little. It was far wiser to trust in Jehovah than in Egypt's army:

> Woe to them that go down to Egypt for help, and rely on horses, and trust in chariots because there are many, and in horsemen because they are very strong, but they look not unto the Holy One of Israel, neither seek Jehovah! Yet he also is wise, and will bring evil, and will not call back his words, but will rise against the house of the evildoers, and against the help of them that work iniquity. Now the Egyptians are men, and not God; and their horses flesh, and not spirit: and when Jehovah shall stretch out his hand, both he that helpeth shall stumble, and he that is helped shall fall, and they all shall be consumed together (Isa. 31:1-3).

Again and again the admonition comes to depend

on God, not man. Egypt represents the material, and in such there is no saving grace. God is the one reliable help, and no matter if we seem completely hedged in by limitation, we should trust Him. In all matters pertaining to outer action, our spiritual teachers urge that we turn to God for guidance and then act as He directs. Only Divine Mind can reveal what is best for here and now.

Isaiah's pleading had little effect, and Judah joined Egypt and neighboring Palestine cities in a rebellion against Assyria. That this was an unwise move was revealed all too soon. Sennacherib had succeeded Sargon II, and within a few years he marched into Palestine, spreading terror throughout the region. Hezekiah trusted in Egypt's promise for assistance, but the weak force furnished by her was quickly defeated by the Assyrians. Sennacherib marched on, and one Judean city after another was plundered and burned. Jerusalem was hurriedly put in a state of siege. However, when the Assyrians reached the walls of the city, no resistance was offered. Hezekiah emptied his treasury, stripped his palace, even took the gold from the doors and pillars of the Temple, and sent the treasure to Sennacherib as a peace offering. For this the Assyrians spared Jerusalem, and Hezekiah was allowed to retain his crown.

For a time Judah was at peace, and when Assyria again tried to gain full control of Judah, Isaiah influenced the King to refuse to surrender, declaring that Jehovah would protect Jerusalem:

Thus saith Jehovah concerning the king of Assyria, He shall not come unto this city, nor shoot an arrow there, neither shall he come before it with shield, nor cast up a mound against it. By the way that he came, by the same shall he return . . . For I will defend this city to save it, for mine own sake, and for my servant David's sake (Isa. 37:33-35).

There are times when we should be nonresistant and times when great firmness is the way of wisdom. Every situation is different, and we should always ask for divine guidance. Isaiah, who represents spiritual understanding, will prompt us to right action if we turn to him. Despite the efforts of Assyrian ambassadors to frighten Hezekiah by saying that the Lord had not saved others and would not save Judah, the King maintained his stand:

And the angel of Jehovah went forth, and smote in the camp of the Assyrians a hundred and fourscore and five thousand; and when men arose early in the morning, behold, these were all dead bodies. So Sennacherib king of Assyria departed, and went and returned, and dwelt at Nineveh (Isa. 37:36, 37).

Whenever we operate in conjunction with divine wisdom we are always preserved and often in ways that it would be impossible to foresee. The smiting of the Assyrian soldiers by the "angel of Jehovah" conveys to us the assurance that, regardless of the seeming strength of opposing forces, the one who heeds the word of the Lord and obeys it will be preserved. On numberless occasions the Bible reiterates that man, functioning *with* God, is invincible; apart from Him, he is the prey of destructive elements.

Later in his reign Hezekiah was taken sick, and Isaiah prophesied that he would die. Hezekiah took his own case to the Lord:

> Remember now, O Jehovah, I beseech thee, how I have walked before thee in truth and with a perfect heart, and have done that which is good in thy sight (Isa. 38:2).

There are times when the law that we have unconsciously set into activity brings dire results unless prompt spiritual steps are taken to avert them. Always we find release if we pray and in faith claim our good. This is what Hezekiah did. Truly, the loving-kindness of Jehovah *"endureth* for ever." The prophet was quick to sense a change, and though on his way out of the palace, he returned to Hezekiah, asserting that the king's days would be prolonged and telling him how to cure his illness.

Throughout this stormy political period the wonderful messages of Isaiah are scattered. He realized that Judah's fate would be similar to that of Israel unless the people relied on Jehovah. Again and again the substance of his words is, "In returning and rest shall ye be saved; in quietness and in confidence shall be your strength" (Isa. 30:5).

Isaiah shared the antipathy of the earlier prophets for the elaborate sacrificial cult of the priests. God does not want empty forms but righteousness, Isaiah declared.

> What unto me is the multitude of your sacrifices? saith Jehovah: I have had enough of the burnt-offerings

of rams, and the fat of fed beasts . . . Bring no more vain oblations; incense is an abomination unto me . . . And when ye spread forth your hands, I will hide mine eyes from you; yea, when ye make many prayers, I will not hear . . . Wash you, make you clean; put away the evil of your doings from before mine eyes; cease to do evil; learn to do well; seek justice, relieve the oppressed . . .

Come now, and let us reason together, saith Jehovah: though your sins be as scarlet, they shall be as white as snow . . . If ye be willing and obedient, ye shall eat the good of the land: but if ye refuse and rebel, ye shall be devoured with the sword (Isa. 1:11, 13, 15-20).

Isaiah gives very helpful and practical advice as to what to do when things in the outer arouse our anger or resentment:

Come, my people, enter thou into thy chambers, and shut thy doors about thee: hide thyself for a little moment, until the indignation be overpast (Isa. 26-20).

The prophet speaks frequently of the remnant that shall preserve the nation. The term remnant, as used by various prophets, referred to the small minority of Jews who understood Jehovah and obeyed Him. These constituted the real strength of Judah. "Except Jehovah of hosts had left unto us a very small remnant, we should have been as Sodom, we should have been like unto Gomorrah" (Isa. 1:9). It was indeed the remnant that returned to Jerusalem after the Babylonian captivity and rebuilt the city and the Temple.

Throughout the ages there has been this spiritual remnant, and today it consists of the truly spiritual-minded people regardless of race, color, or creed.

They are those who acknowledge God as the one presence and power and whose lives express the spiritual qualities inherent in all people. Isaiah described their mode of activity as: "The remnant . . . shall . . . take root downward, and bear fruit upward" (Isa. 37:31). Such action is always characteristic of those who are established in spiritual consciousness. To take root downward means to retire to the inner realm of our being where contact is made with God. This results in bearing fruit upward, the demonstration. The remnant always works this way, from the within out. They seek first "his kingdom, and his righteousness" (Matt. 6:33), content that the things shall be added in good time.

Isaiah foretells the coming of the Messiah. The Hebrew word for Messiah and the Greek word *Christos* have the same meaning, that is, the anointed one. Perhaps the loveliest and most familiar of Isaiah's prophecies concerning the Messiah is:

> The people that walked in darkness have seen a great light: they that dwelt in the land of the shadow of death, upon them hath the light shined. . . . For unto us a child is born, unto us a son is given; and the government shall be upon his shoulder: and his name shall be called Wonderful, Counsellor, Mighty God, Everlasting Father, Prince of Peace. Of the increase of his government and of peace there shall be no end (Isa. 9:2, 6, 7).

The Messianic prophecies found fulfillment in Jesus of Nazareth. In Him was the full expression of the Christ or spiritual nature of man. However, we should not think of the prophecies as ending with

Jesus. The Messiah (Christ) is to unfold in the lives of all when they shall, through prayer and righteousness, unify their consciousness with the Spirit of truth or God indwelling.

As the Everlasting Father, the Prince of Peace rules the hearts of men, Isaiah visions a world of love and harmony:

The wolf shall dwell with the lamb, and the leopard shall lie down with the kid; and the calf and the young lion and the fatling together; and a little child shall lead them. . . . They shall not hurt nor destroy in all my holy mountain; for the earth shall be full of the knowledge of Jehovah, as the waters cover the sea (Isa. 11:6-9).

While all the prophets denounced the people for their sins, they spoke in the hope of reformation, knowing full well the ability of man to mend his ways and the willingness of God to forgive. His grace is ever available to us, and Isaiah, speaking His word, gives voice to the beautiful promise:

And the work of righteousness shall be peace; and the effect of righteousness, quietness and confidence for ever. And my people shall abide in a peaceable habitation, and in safe dwellings, and in quiet resting-places (Isa. 32:17, 18).

In every age of the world's history, men's hearts have yearned for such fulfillment. They have longed for quietness, confidence, peace. These are ever dependent for their manifestation on the "work of righteousness," which this great prophet, more than seven hundred years before Jesus, urged men to perform. Blessed indeed are those inspired men who have eyes to see, ears to hear, and the will to do.

Micah (735-700 B.C.)

A few years after Isaiah entered upon his prophetic mission, another prophet, whose name was Micah, appeared in Judah. Micah was a native of Maresheth-Gath, a rural town near the city of Gath. He also had high conceptions of the nature of God and of the obligation resting upon his people. Between Micah's messages and those of Isaiah there is much similarity of thought and even of expression, showing that Micah was greatly influenced by Isaiah. But while Isaiah's sphere of activity was in Jerusalem, where he was the adviser of kings, Micah was a peasant farmer and in close touch with the lower classes. Undoubtedly Micah played a large part in inspiring the masses to cooperate in the religious reforms of Hezekiah.

Micah added nothing essentially new to the prophetic utterances of Isaiah, yet he gave to humanity what is perhaps the most perfect definition of true religion:

He [Jehovah] hath showed thee, O man, what is good; and what doth Jehovah require of thee, but to do justly, and to love kindness, and to walk humbly with thy God? (Micah 6:8).

The very simplicity of the words confounds the worldly wise, but provides an adequate pattern for spiritual thought and conduct for those who in simple faith believe in and love their Father-God.

CHAPTER XIV

Prophets of the Seventh Century B.C.

II Kings 21-25; II Chronicles 33-36; Zephaniah;
Jeremiah; Nahum; Habakkuk

T HE GOOD KING Hezekiah was on the throne
of Judah at the beginning of the seventh
century, and when he died in 696 B.C. his
son Manasseh succeeded him. Manasseh reigned for
fifty-five years and "did that which was evil in the
sight of Jehovah" (II Kings 21:2) by permitting
a return to Canaanite idolatry. He also opened wide
the door to Assyrian customs "and worshipped all
the hosts of heaven, and served them" (II Kings
21:3).

During these years Judah reached a new low
level in apostasy. The labors of the great eighth
century prophets, Amos, Hosea, I Isaiah, and Micah,
seem to have been utterly unavailing. But a seed
once sown bears fruit in time, and after the short
reign of Amon, Manasseh's son, Josiah came to the
throne. He ruled from 640 to 608 B.C.

As a young king Josiah instituted religious reforms beginning with the repair of the Temple,
which had fallen into a sad state. The finding of the
"book of the law" (II Kings 22:8) that we know as
Deuteronomy, evidently written some half century
before and hid in the Temple during the evil reign of
Manasseh, resulted in a wholehearted religious revival. The discovery of a document, supposedly writ-

ten by Moses, turned the attention of king and people in a very direct way to Jehovah. Moses had promised the Children of Israel great good in the land of Canaan if they obeyed the commandments of the Lord:

And it shall come to pass, if thou shalt hearken diligently unto the voice of Jehovah thy God, to observe to do all his commandments which I command thee this day, that Jehovah thy God will set thee on high above all the nations of the earth: and all these blessings shall come upon thee, and overtake thee, if thou shalt hearken unto the voice of Jehovah thy God. Blessed shalt thou be in the city, and blessed shalt thou be in the field (Deut. 28:1-3).

With Egypt to the south and powerful Assyria to the north (to whom Judah had been paying yearly tribute since the time of Ahaz) the Jews were threatened with grave danger. They longed to feel secure and to prosper once more. The words of their great leader Moses brought to mind that blessings would come if they would "hearken diligently unto the voice of Jehovah." Therefore, the finding of the book of the law in the Temple instigated a revival of the worship of the Lord. Unfortunately, it proved to be one of those surface reformations that influenced outer acts, as evidenced by the destruction of altars to foreign gods, but it did not penetrate the consciousness of the masses. However, the official priests and prophets of the Temple were elated. They declared that Judah was safe for she was under the protection of Jehovah. There was a current belief that the "day of Jehovah" (Zech. 14:1) was close at hand when Judah would gain her complete freedom and be restored to a position of power among the nations. To this belief, well-sounding to the ears of Judah's people, the first of the seventh century prophets took exception.

Zephaniah (about 626 B.C.)

Zephaniah announced that the "day of Jehovah" would come but that it would not be the sort of day the Jews expected. It would be a time of reckoning and doom for the unrepentant. Jehovah was about to punish iniquity, said the prophet, not only among the Jews but in the countries of Assyria, Philistia, Moab, and Ammon. Only the righteous would escape. Zephaniah counseled,

> Seek ye Jehovah, all ye meek of the earth, that have kept his ordinances; seek righteousness, seek meekness: it may be ye will be hid in the day of Jehovah's anger (Zeph. 2:3).

The name Zephaniah means "Jehovah has hidden," and symbolizes "Truth active in the consciousness of the individual but hidden from the outer, sense phase of his being" (M.D. 693). This meaning is borne out by the message of Zephaniah, who realized that righteousness alone can save man. When we are functioning in sense consciousness, we have no understanding of this. It is hid from us. The people of Zephaniah's day were laboring under the false assumption that Jehovah would save them because nominally He was their God, as some Christians today hold that their salvation is assured because they accept Jesus as their redeemer. But when Truth becomes active in consciousness (Zephaniah comes forth), it is understood that worship, manifesting in righteous living, is all that can protect.

Zephaniah was a stern and somewhat puritanical prophet. An inner revelation of God's law enables us to discern wherein we have fallen short. After experiencing it, we are liable to be positive in our denunciation of evil. Like Zephaniah, we know that deliverance is ours if we will return to the Lord:

> Therefore wait ye for me, saith Jehovah, until the day that I rise up to the prey . . . The remnant of Israel shall not do iniquity, nor speak lies . . . for they shall feed and lie down, and none shall make them afraid (Zeph. 3:8, 13).

Jeremiah (626-580 B.C.)

The Book of Jeremiah is the longest of the prophetical books to be written by one person. It is also the most personal, revealing clearly the character and ideals of the prophet. Jeremiah's sermons were gathered together by Baruch, his friend and secretary, and no effort was made to put them in chronological or topical order. In the Authorized and the American Standard versions of the Bible, the Book of Jeremiah is not easy to read, and some modern scholars have rearranged the material. Also, the political situation of Judah at that time was so intertwined with the prophetic messages that without some knowledge of the historical background, certain parts of the book are unintelligible.

Jeremiah belonged to a priestly family of Anathoth, a village some six miles north of Jerusalem. He was a man of education and property. To him fell the most difficult task of any of the Hebrew prophets, for he spoke during the last half century of Judah's existence as a nation. He is often referred to as the "Prophet of Doom" because the greater part of his message predicts the hardships to overtake the Jews for their transgressions. However, when the situation he faced is considered, it can readily be seen that words less vigorous in tone would have been ignored.

Jeremiah represents "spiritual faith demanding that all religious thoughts be true in observance of divine law" (M.D. 338). Before faith is firmly established we may have a sense of timidity as regards our ability to teach Truth; we may shrink from the task we intuitively feel is ours. Jeremiah tells of his call to prophetic service in the first chapter of his book. When it was revealed to him that he was to be a prophet "unto the nations" (Jer. 1:5), his response was "Behold, I know not how to speak; for I am a child" (Jer. 1:6). The claim of inadequacy was refuted by the Lord:

Say not, I am a child; for to whomsoever I shall send thee thou shalt go, and whatsoever I shall command thee thou shalt speak. Be not afraid because of them; for I am with thee to deliver thee . . . Then Jehovah put forth his hand, and touched my mouth . . . Behold, I have put my words in thy mouth: see, I have this day set thee over the nations and over the kingdoms, to pluck up and to break down and to destroy and to overthrow, to build and to plant (Jer. 1:7-10).

When we are in the Jeremiah state of consciousness and aware of a definite call from the Lord, all our timidity vanishes and we are courageous in testifying to spiritual reality. His was a twofold mission, to destroy error and to establish Truth. Error is destroyed by our faithful practice of denials, and Truth is established as we consistently affirm the presence and power of God.

Jeremiah plunged into his work without delay. His early sermons coming during the reign of Josiah urged a prompt and effective repentance and the institution of a religion of the spirit, not of the letter. It is not enough to cease doing evil (and destroy altars to false gods); it is necessary to be active in doing good. Jeremiah was encouraged by the sweeping reforms made by Josiah and hoped they might be permanent. However, political changes, beginning in 612 B.C., brought about changes for the worse on the religious scene. In that year the Assyrians were conquered by the Chaldeans. Egypt, making a bid for world power, attacked Judah, and Josiah was killed at the battle of Megiddo in 608 B.C. For a few years Judah was the vassal of Egypt, but at Carchemish, Necho of Egypt suffered defeat at the hands of Nebuchadnezzar, king of Chaldea. Thus Chaldea, or Babylonia as it is more often referred to in Scripture, became the overlord of Judah.

Jehoiakim followed his father Josiah on the

throne of Judah, and Jeremiah soon perceived that
the nation was doomed, for Jehoiakim was not the
man to uphold a spiritual regime. True, Jehovah was
still worshiped but so were other gods. Jeremiah began to prophesy the country's fall. This brought on
scathing denunciations from Temple priests and
prophets. They declared that Jerusalem could not be
conquered, for it contained the Temple, which was
the abiding place of Jehovah, and He would protect the city. Jeremiah insisted that safety lay not in
the Temple but only in the people's understanding
of Jehovah and conformity to His will:

> Thus saith Jehovah of hosts, the God of Israel, Amend
> your ways and your doings . . . if ye thoroughly execute
> justice between a man and his neighbor; if ye oppress not
> the sojourner, the fatherless, and the widow, and shed
> not innocent blood in this place, neither walk after other
> gods to your own hurt: then will I cause you to dwell
> in this place, in the land that I gave to your fathers, from
> of old even for evermore (Jer. 7:3-7).

Jeremiah also advised co-operation with Babylonia. To resist would be ruinous, he insisted. Such
counsel seemed traitorous to the political authorities,
including the King. They wanted to rebel against
Babylonia and longed to be told that the Lord would
help them. Jeremiah knew that nonresistance was the
way of wisdom. There are times when certain causes
have been set in activity and certain results are inevitable unless we can fully unify ourselves with
God. This is difficult unless one has established a
spiritual consciousness. The Jews of that day, like so

many of us today, wanted to live their own lives irrespective of the commandments of the Lord, and yet in this time of emergency they hoped He would provide security.

Only as we live in harmony with the spiritual forces of our being can we expect the good of God to be manifested in our affairs. There are occasions when conscious or unconscious disobedience to Him produces disastrous conditions, and these we should learn to meet wisely. For example, we do not believe that lack of substance is God's will for anyone, yet we sometimes have a financial crisis to meet. What should we do? Resist the situation, blame others for our difficulty, or try to force plenty by begging people for help?

There is a spiritual way of meeting such a problem. It consists of taking a passive or nonresistant attitude toward lack but, on the other hand, taking a very positive attitude toward God. Jeremiah tried to show his people that it would be unwise to rebel against Babylonia, that they should build up such spiritual defenses in consciousness that they could meet a destructive condition in a constructive manner. When in the midst of hardship we can learn to trust God, He will deliver us. The Jews learned this lesson later, during the years of the Exile, but when Jeremiah was preaching to them, they thought he was disloyal both to Jehovah and to his country.

Thus Jeremiah was alienated from political as well as religious groups. His neighbors in Anathoth tried to prevent him from preaching. The official priests mobbed him and put him in the stocks. The King's anger finally forced him into hiding for a time. Jeremiah was bewildered by these bitter experiences. To the best of his understanding he was speaking the word of the Lord and he asked of Him, "Wherefore doth the way of the wicked prosper? wherefore are all they at ease that deal very treacherously?" (Jer. 12:1). Such questions come to the mind of every conscientious person who seems to be persecuted for righteousness' sake. It was revealed to Jeremiah that though he would meet even greater trials, the Lord would strengthen and sustain him.

King Jehoiakim, influenced by the pro-Egyptian party in Jerusalem and deaf to Jeremiah's counsel, refused to pay tribute to Babylonia. In 597 B.C. Nebuchadnezzar sent an army to besiege Jerusalem. Jehoiakim died as the army advanced on the city and was succeeded by his son Jehoiachin. Without power to protect Jerusalem the young King surrendered, and he, the royal family, the court, and thousands of the upper-class Jews were transported to Babylonia. However, the King's prompt surrender secured a relatively mild punishment for Judah. Nebuchadnezzar placed Zedekiah, another son of Josiah, on the throne. Though the Babylonians partially stripped the Temple they did not destroy it, and the Jews were permitted to continue worship there.

It was during this period that Jeremiah questioned the Lord regarding his mission. When we do the best we know and results are unsatisfactory, we are apt to feel that God has forsaken us. Jeremiah cried:

O Jehovah, thou knowest; remember me, and visit me, and avenge me of my persecutors; take me not away in thy longsuffering: know that for thy sake I have suffered reproach. Thy words were found, and I did eat them; and thy words were unto me a joy and the rejoicing of my heart . . . Why is my pain perpetual, and my wound incurable, which refuseth to be healed? wilt thou indeed be unto me as a deceitful *brook*, as waters that fail? (Jer. 15: 15-18).

The Lord's response to this heartfelt cry was prompt:

Therefore thus saith Jehovah, If thou return, then will I bring thee again, that thou mayest stand before me; and if thou take forth the precious from the vile, thou shalt be as my mouth . . . And I will make thee unto this people a fortified brazen wall; and they shall fight against thee, but they shall not prevail against thee; for I am with thee to save thee and to deliver thee (Jer. 15:19, 20).

Note that Jeremiah did not take his complaint to the people nor keep it to himself in inner resentment. He cast his burden directly upon the Lord, which is what we should do. Then it was revealed to Jeremiah that his only task was to keep in close contact with the source of strength, to learn to separate essentials from nonessentials, "the precious from the vile." If he would do so, he would be as "a fortified brazen wall," against which nothing could prevail. Everyone who tries to be true to the highest he knows has periods of intense discouragement and cries, "My God, my God, why hast thou forsaken me?" (Matt. 27:46) but in returning to God he finds strength and reassurance.

To the captive Jews in Babylonia, Jeremiah wrote a letter giving excellent advice on how to meet this trial.

> Thus saith Jehovah . . . Build ye houses, and dwell in them; and plant gardens, and eat the fruit of them. Take ye wives, and beget sons and daughters . . . And seek the peace of the city whither I have caused you to be carried away captive, and pray unto Jehovah for it; for in the peace thereof shall ye have peace (Jer. 29:5-7).

So does the spiritual self speak to us, bidding us live constructively whatever the condition. Jeremiah prophesied a long captivity, but he reminded the captives that there is mercy in the heart of the Almighty and they could find their God (or their good) if they sought Him diligently:

> For thus saith Jehovah, After seventy years are accomplished for Babylon, I will visit you, and perform my good word toward you, in causing you to return to this place. For I know the thoughts that I think toward you, saith Jehovah, thoughts of peace, and not of evil, to give you hope in your latter end. And ye shall call upon me, and ye shall go and pray unto me, and I will hearken unto you. And ye shall seek me, and find me, when ye shall search for me with all your heart (Jer. 29:10-13).

With the sorrow of the deportation of their king (Jehoiachin) and thousands of their countrymen lying heavily on their hearts, the people of Judah blamed the state of affairs on two things: first, the might of Babylonia, and second, the sins of their fathers. Such is a common fault of human nature. It makes no difference what we call our foe—a country, economic conditions, fate, or luck—we are still shifting the blame to the power of adverse conditions. Also we are prone to place the responsibility for our deficiencies on the "iniquity of the fathers" (Exod. 20:5), declaring that we inherited diseases or undesirable characteristics from them, or that they failed to provide the proper education or environment necessary to our well-being.

Jeremiah was not the first teacher of the Jews to point out the need of individual righteousness, but he gave it new and added emphasis. He declared that his people were in dire straits because they themselves had been remiss: "My people have committed two evils [saith Jehovah]: they have forsaken me, the fountain of living waters, and hewed them out cisterns, broken cisterns, that can hold no water" (Jer. 2:13). We must have something in which to place our faith, and when we turn from God (forsake the spiritual), we invariably turn to the mortal, which is ever inadequate (a broken cistern that can hold no water). This and this alone is the cause of our troubles.

King Zedekiah, who had been placed on the throne of Judah by Nebuchadnezzar, proved to be weak and inexperienced. As the leaders among the professional, intellectual, and religious classes had been removed to Babylonia, Zedekiah was forced to depend on inferior advisers. These favored a revolt against Babylonia by a refusal to pay tribute. To this Jeremiah was strongly opposed. His word was disregarded, however, and the result was a prompt attack on Jerusalem by Nebuchadnezzar. Jeremiah was imprisoned on a charge of treason. Though released after a short time, he was then thrown into a well to starve. Only the secret support of Zedekiah and a friend saved him from death. He was kept a prisoner in the palace until Jerusalem fell.

During this time Jeremiah wrote the messages included in the 30th through the 33d chapter of his book, known as the Book of Hope. In these beautiful portions there is no denunciation of the people for their sins. Their punishment was upon them, and Jeremiah, with all the love he felt for his God and his countrymen, sought to comfort them by prophesying that the nation would rise again:

> For, lo, the days come, saith Jehovah, that I will turn again the captivity of my people Israel and Judah . . . and I will cause them to return to the land that I gave to their fathers, and they shall possess it (Jer. 30:3).

These chapters are filled with encouragement, and in the 31st there is the promise of the new covenant:

> Behold, the days come, saith Jehovah, that I will make a new covenant with the house of Israel, and with the house of Judah . . . I will put my law in their inward parts, and in their heart will I write it; and I will be their God, and they shall be my people. And they shall teach no more every man his neighbor, and every man his

brother, saying, Know Jehovah; for they shall all know me, from the least of them unto the greatest of them . . . for I will forgive their iniquity, and their sin will I remember no more (Jer. 31:31-34).

When Nebuchadnezzar's troops finally breached the walls of Jerusalem and razed the Temple, Jeremiah was released from imprisonment by a Babylonian officer and given permission to choose whether he would remain in Jerusalem, move to another section of Judah, or join the captives to be taken to Babylon. The prophet chose to remain in the half-destroyed Holy City, giving his support to Gedaliah, the Jewish governor appointed by Nebuchadnezzar. When Gedaliah was murdered a few years later, Jeremiah was forced to flee to Egypt with a company of Jews. Tradition says that he met his death at the hands of his own people because of his denunciation of their worship of Egyptian gods.

Were we to judge the life of Jeremiah by the events that filled it, it would seem tragic indeed. But could any man who knew the Lord so well have aught in his heart but the peace that passes understanding? He strove always to turn men to God, and in the utterance of such messages as his, his spirit must have soared on high. Surely Jeremiah is one of the few who, failing to accomplish their hearts' desire, still refuse to surrender their own integrity. "To strive, to seek, to find, and not to yield," is a great accomplishment.

Nahum (612 B.C.)

The prophet Nahum began his prophetic career

during the latter years of Josiah's reign. His book is
unique among Hebrew prophetical works, as he does
not mention the transgressions of his people. His
messages consist of a description of the fall of the
great Assyrian capital Nineveh, the foe of Judah.
He believed that the greatness of Judah would be
restored when Assyria was conquered.

Nahum gives a vivid description of the destruction of the wicked city, and brings out the idea that
God's moral judgment must be upon all who oppose
His law. As a dramatic poem his book is a magnificent piece of writing, but it is spiritual in content
only to the extent that it draws attention to the truth
that wickedness invariably leads to annihilation.

Habakkuk (612-600 B.C.)

It is thought that sometime between these dates
the prophet Habakkuk raised his voice in Jerusalem,
the majority of his messages probably coming during
the turbulent reign of Jehoiakim. In contrast to the
prophets who spoke to the people in an attempt to
turn them to Jehovah, Habakkuk addressed himself
to the Lord. He was an earnest seeker of Truth and
could not reconcile his own high conception of God
with the prevailing evil in Judah. How, he asked,
can a God of justice permit the wicked to "compass
about the righteous; therefore justice goeth forth
perverted" (Hab. 1:4)? The answer he received was
to the effect that the Babylonians would execute
Jehovah's vengeance. But this brought another question to the prophet's lips: How could the Baby-

lonians, who were themselves wicked, be used by the Lord? To this Jehovah replied that the Babylonians, though temporarily mighty, were sure to work out their own punishment. "The righteous shall live by his faith" (Hab. 2:4), waiting patiently and steadfastly for the God of all men to give to each according as his work shall be. Habakkuk was reminded, as we so often are, "Jehovah is in his holy temple: let all the earth keep silence before him" (Hab. 2:20).

The name Habakkuk means "embracing, infolding." Metaphysically he signifies:

The clearness of vision in us that, looking into the working of the thoughts of our consciousness, foresees their fruition and holds tightly to *(embraces)* that which is good and true, while it *wrestles,* or *struggles,* with the error in an attempt to purge it out (M.D. 244).

We are like Habakkuk when, in all earnestness, we question the operation of divine law but, upon receiving the illumination that we should live by faith, come to the great realization with which Habakkuk's message closes:

Jehovah, the Lord, is my strength;
And he maketh my feet like hinds' *feet,*
And will make me to walk upon my high places
(Hab. 3:19).

CHAPTER XV

Prophets of the Exile

Ezekiel;
Isaiah 40-55

TO THE TEN THOUSAND Jewish captives transported to Babylonia in 597 B.C., another group was added in 586 B.C. For convenience the date 586 B.C. is given as the beginning of the period of fifty years known as the Babylonian captivity, or the Exile. The Jews were settled on the banks of one of the many canals in Babylonia, called the Chebar. They were in no sense slaves and were given freedom to manage their private affairs, engage in business, and worship as they chose. Nebuchadnezzar seems to have had no hatred for them and destroyed their country only because the Jews would not be subservient to him.

Considered spiritually, the Babylonian captivity represents the state of outer limitation brought about by a departure from spiritual consciousness. The name Babylon, which comes from Babel, means confusion. It typifies the mixed or confused state of consciousness resulting when sense thoughts dominate the mind. Such a state places us in captivity. Our homeland is Jerusalem (signifying spiritual peace), and when we are separated from it there is a feeling of loneliness and heartache. We do not like the "foreign land" of Babylonia (confusion) and yearn to return to our native state, peace with God. The

137th Psalm is a product of this period and expresses the homesickness of man for his spiritual home:

By the rivers of Babylon,
There we sat down, yea, we wept,
When we remembered Zion.
Upon the willows in the midst thereof
We hanged up our harps.
For there they that led us captive required of us songs,
And they that wasted us *required of us* mirth, *saying,*
Sing us one of the songs of Zion.
How shall we sing Jehovah's song
In a foreign land?
If I forget thee, O Jerusalem,
Let my right hand forget *her skill.*
Let my tongue cleave to the roof of my mouth,
If I remember thee not;
If I prefer not Jerusalem
Above my chief joy.

We can never be released from bondage until we change our consciousness. There is always a way to do this, for God provides for us regardless of the distressing condition into which we have fallen. It was the mission of the two great prophets of the Exile, Ezekiel and Deutero-Isaiah, to help the Jews (and us) rise to a higher plane of thought.

Ezekiel (597-570 B.C.)

Ezekiel was among the captives transported to Babylonia in 597 B.C., and he began his ministry some four years later, which was before Jerusalem was destroyed and while Jeremiah was still preaching. Ezekiel was the son of Buzi, and a priest who was to become a prophet also. Ezekiel represents:

That in us which relies on Spirit and encourages us to place our full trust in Jehovah, that the Lord Jehovah (the spiritual I AM in us) may become the keeper of our sheep (our spiritual thoughts). Ezekiel was an enthusiast. His mind was open and alive to things spiritual. He shows us how to demonstrate strength (M.D. 212).

In times of distress we need just the consciousness Ezekiel symbolizes. He will come forth to instruct and guide us that we may have the strength to lift up our eyes to God. In the upward sight lies our ability to meet a hard condition in a spiritual manner.

Ezekiel's call to prophetic service came in vision form. "The heavens were opened, and I saw visions of God" (Ezek. 1:1). Out of a luminous cloud there appeared four living creatures and wheels with rims filled with eyes. From the complicated symbolism of the vision, great spiritual truths emerge. God is transcendent, above all, but God is also immanent, within all. "The wheel within a wheel" signifies the life of man within the life of the divine. The action of the living creatures is symbolic of man's unfoldment. "And they went every one straight forward: whither the spirit was to go, they went; they turned not when they went" (Ezek. 1:12).

It often seems that we take devious paths that lead to frustration and sorrow. But is it not true that man, no matter how far removed he may be from the spiritual, goes straight forward in the only way he can at the time? As we realize this, we are less apt to condemn others for their sins of omission or commission. Each man moves according to the light he has, and, somehow, someday, each will perceive the light of Spirit and follow it. Ezekiel meant to convey the idea to his people that though the Exile seemed a hardship, it was still a "straight" way and the Lord was with them. The living creature, man, is the son of almighty God, and he goes ever forward. A seeming turn is merely the verdict of eyes that cannot see.

As the vision faded, Ezekiel fell upon his face. "Stand upon thy feet, and I will speak with thee" (Ezek. 2:1), commanded Jehovah. An upright position implies an upright consciousness. The feet often symbolize understanding. We must rise in consciousness, stand erect, before we can hear God's commission and go forth to fulfill it. The prophet was given a roll of a book and told to eat it. "And it was in my mouth as honey for sweetness" (Ezek. 3:3), he records. We are to eat, to appropriate, the divine word, and it is sweet to the consecrated man. Then Ezekiel was commissioned to speak to the house of Israel, and was assured thus: "I will open thy mouth, and thou shalt say unto them, Thus saith the Lord Jehovah" (Ezek. 3:27). He was also to be a watchman over his people, warning the wicked and comforting the righteous.

Ezekiel was truly an enthusiast and he employed dramatic ways of giving his messages. Sometimes he told of visions, such as the valley of dry bones; sometimes he used symbolic actions, such as rationing his food and water to scant quantities to signify the meagerness of provisions in Jerusalem during the siege of the city. He also used allegories to convey his meaning, such as likening Jerusalem and its sinful people to a worthless wild vine that must be cast into the fire. He employed every means of teaching to awaken the Jews to a realization that the Captivity was the result of their iniquities, but that Jehovah is a God of mercy and if they would trust and obey Him their restoration was certain.

Ezekiel made much of the principle of individual responsibility. He asked, "What mean ye, that ye use this proverb concerning the land of Israel, saying, The fathers have eaten sour grapes, and the children's teeth are set on edge?" (Ezek. 18:2). Jeremiah had refuted the erroneous belief that man suffers for the sins of his fathers, and Ezekiel amplified it:

> As I live, saith the Lord Jehovah . . . Behold, all souls are mine; as the soul of the father, so also the soul of the son is mine: the soul that sinneth, it shall die (Ezek. 18:4).

Ezekiel taught that man's standing before God is not to be determined by his parents or even by his own past. How essential for us to know this! Frequently we labor under the belief that limitations are inflicted upon us because of others' deficiencies. To perceive that nobody or nothing can keep us from our good is indeed a freeing thought. We have to release also the belief that our own past wrongdoing can hold us in bondage. We have all made mistakes, some very serious ones, but whenever we sincerely repent and ask God's forgiveness, it is forthcoming. To contend that we suffer for the misdeeds of others leads to self-pity. To hold that our own past misdeeds hang like the sword of Damocles over our heads leads to self-condemnation. Neither has any place in the mind of the one who would attune himself to God. Ezekiel suggests what to do:

Return ye, and turn yourselves from all your transgressions; so iniquity shall not be your ruin. . . . for why will ye die, O house of Israel? For I have no pleasure in the death of him that dieth, saith the Lord Jehovah: wherefore turn yourselves, and live (Ezek. 18:30-32).

Any teacher's most effective teaching lies in his own actions. "If ye know these things, blessed are ye if ye do them" (John 13:17). To talk is easy, but to perform in line with our talk is sometimes very difficult. Ezekiel was able to do this. In the midst of his ministry he met a great sorrow in the death of his wife, and the word of the Lord came to him:

Thou shalt neither mourn nor weep, neither shall thy tears run down. Sigh, but not aloud, make no mourning for the dead; bind thy headtire upon thee, and put thy shoes upon thy feet, and cover not thy lips, and eat not the bread of men (Ezek. 24:16, 17).

The prophet obeyed the Lord's instruction and expressed great fortitude as he said:

So I spake unto the people in the morning; and at even my wife died; and I did in the morning as I was commanded (Ezek. 24:18).

When his companions asked for an explanation

of his courage, Ezekiel told them that they, too, would have sorrow to meet when Jerusalem fell. The Holy City was as precious to them as his wife was to him. Nevertheless they should refrain from mourning and set themselves to the task at hand.

May we benefit by the prophet's word and deed. Grief is apt to overwhelm us when a loved one passes on. Instead we should hold fast to our God and meet the condition bravely. There is work to be done by each person just where he is. To give way to mourning harms us and does not benefit our loved one who has stepped into another mansion of the Father's house. With the Father's help we can transmute our love into service to those about us. This is our highest duty and bespeaks a living faith in a merciful God.

At times the people became very despondent, for the Exile seemed a harsh punishment. They complained of being naught but dried bones. Ezekiel then told them of his vision. He saw a great valley filled with the bones of an army, and Jehovah asked, "Can these bones live?" (Ezek. 37:3). Ezekiel was doubtful. Whereupon Jehovah bade him prophesy to the bones that He would cause them to live and would clothe them with human bodies. The prophet obeyed, the dried bones stirred, and bodies were reformed. Yet they lacked life and Jehovah commanded:

Prophesy unto the wind, prophesy, son of man, and say to the wind, Thus saith the Lord Jehovah: Come from the four winds, O breath, and breathe upon these slain, that they may live. So I prophesied as he commanded me, and the breath came into them, and they lived, and stood up upon their feet, an exceeding great army (Ezek. 37:9, 10).

The prophet's vision and its meaning were obvious: could not Jehovah create the nation anew? "And I will put my Spirit in you, and ye shall live, and I will place you in your own land: and ye shall know that I, Jehovah, have spoken it and performed it" (Ezek. 37:14).

Sometimes we view ourselves as dried bones, inert, fruitless. Cannot our own indwelling Spirit breathe into us? A sick body reanimated and made strong, lack in affairs restored to plenty, and sorrow elevated to joy are evidences of the power of the Almighty functioning through those who believe and let the marvelous life force within them do its vitalizing work.

By his messages Ezekiel put new hope into the exiles. He predicted that the nation would be re-established and that the Jews in Babylonia were to become the nucleus of the restored state. Thus saith Jehovah:

For I will take you from among the nations, and gather you out of all the countries, and will bring you into your own land. And I will sprinkle clean water upon you, and ye shall be clean: from all your filthiness, and from all your idols, will I cleanse you. A new heart also will I give you, and a new spirit will I put within you; and I will take away the stony heart out of your flesh . . . And I will put my Spirit within you, and cause you to walk in my statutes, and ye shall keep mine ordinances, and do them. And ye shall dwell in the land that I gave to your fathers;

and ye shall be my people, and I will be your God (Ezek. 36:24-28).

Ezekiel's was a firm and wise leadership. As the quality of spiritual strength that he represents is established in consciousness, we are able to rise above the limitations of a present state and enthusiastically declare the righteous outworking of all our affairs.

Deutero-Isaiah (546-538 B.C.)
Isaiah 40-55

Nothing is known of the life of the prophet whose words are contained in these chapters of The Book of Isaiah, not even his name. It is supposed that he was a Jew born during the Exile, but who his parents were, what the conditions of his life were, whether he was old or young, or how he was called by the Lord, remains a mystery. He had the wisdom of age, the vitality of youth, and was truly a God-intoxicated man. From a literary standpoint his work is unsurpassed in beauty, and his words are familiar to every seeker after God. He is known as II Isaiah or Deutero-Isaiah. His messages deal little with the iniquities of his people, emphasizing rather the love, compassion, forgiveness, and redemptive power of the Almighty.

When this spiritual seer began his ministry the Jews had been in Babylonia for about forty years. It had been some twenty-four years since Ezekiel had been a tower of strength to them, and during this interim the Jews became disheartened and discouraged. It seemed as if the day of their deliverance would never come. We have much the same feeling when a condition of limitation holds us in spite of our hope and even expectation that release should come. The time was ripe for just such inspiration and hope as Deutero-Isaiah gave. His book is divided into two sections: chapters 40-48 portray an omnipotent God ready to redeem His promises to the Jews, and chapters 49-55 describe the Servant of Jehovah and the future glory of Jerusalem.

The opening words of the message of Deutero-Isaiah breathe consolation and hope:

Comfort ye, comfort ye my people, saith your God. Speak ye comfortably to Jerusalem; and cry unto her, that her warfare is accomplished, that her iniquity is pardoned, that she hath received of Jehovah's hand double for all her sins (Isa. 40: 1, 2).

Before we can begin to move out of a restricted condition of affairs, a change must take place in consciousness. A sense of peace and assurance should come to heart and mind, a realization that there is forgiveness from the God whose law we have unconsciously or deliberately violated. Then we are ready for constructive action. This action Deutero-Isaiah specifies as:

Prepare ye in the wilderness the way of Jehovah; make level in the desert a highway for our God. Every valley shall be exalted, and every mountain and hill shall be made low; and the uneven shall be made level, and the rough places plain: and the glory of Jehovah shall be revealed, and all flesh shall see it together; for the mouth of Jehovah hath spoken it (Isa. 40:3-5).

To prepare ourselves to receive always consists of letting the divine idea come into the mind. A confused state of consciousness may be likened to a wilderness or a desert, and we are to make way in that for the word of the Lord. If we do so, "every valley shall be exalted" (the lower strata of thought raised up), a balanced state of mind reached (the "uneven shall be made level"), and "the glory of Jehovah shall be revealed" (we shall become aware of Spirit as our freedom and power).

These verses set the keynote for the remainder of the prophet's message. We may have an intellectual appreciation of his words and revel in the beauty of them, but unless we accept what he says and do it, we cannot receive the inspiration that lifts us on high.

Behold, the Lord Jehovah will come as a mighty one, and his arm will rule for him: Behold, his reward is with him, and his recompense before him. He will feed his flock like a shepherd, he will gather the lambs in his arm, and carry them in his bosom . . . Hast thou not known? hast thou not heard? The everlasting God, Jehovah, the Creator of the ends of the earth, fainteth not, neither is weary; there is no searching of his understanding. He giveth power to the faint; and to him that hath no might he increaseth strength. Even the youths shall faint and be weary, and the young men shall utterly fall: but they that wait for Jehovah shall renew their strength; they shall mount up with wings as eagles; they shall run, and not be weary; they shall walk, and not faint (Isa. 40:10, 11, 28-31).

Like a chorus in this divine chant come the oft-repeated words, "I am Jehovah, and there is none else; besides me there is no God" (Isa. 45:5). Frequently there seems to be a power adverse to good or God: sickness may reign in body, poverty or unhappiness in affairs. May we listen to this mighty prophet who declares: "There is no God else besides me" (Isa. 45:21).

The poor and needy seek water, and there is none, and their tongue faileth for thirst; I, Jehovah, will answer them, I, the God of Israel, will not forsake them. I will open rivers on the bare heights, and fountains in the midst of the valleys; I will make the wilderness a pool of water, and the dry land springs of water (Isa. 41:17, 18).

We long for the living water that alone can assuage our inner thirst. "I will open rivers on the bare heights" (the mind devoid of enlightening ideas) "and fountains in the midst of the valleys" (the low or difficult places through which we sometimes walk).

On and on throughout these chapters are the wonderful promises of God:

I will go before thee, and make the rough places smooth; I will break in pieces the doors of brass, and cut in sunder the bars of iron (Isa. 45:2).

How many times we need to affirm the following familiar statement of Truth based on the foregoing Scripture, *"The Spirit of the Lord goes before me and makes easy and successful my way."* How many times we should declare that the Father indwelling dissolves and dissipates the hard-and-fast limitations that seem like "doors of brass," and "bars of iron."

The culmination of all the promises heard by Deutero-Isaiah in the quietness of his own being and proclaimed in moving words is the command, "Look unto me, and be ye saved, all the ends of the earth; for I am God, and there is none else" (Isa. 45:22).

For all eternity there is only one Saviour, one Redeemer for any human lack. "Look unto me."

At the time Deutero-Isaiah was giving comfort and enlightenment to his fellow captives, Cyrus, king of Persia, was rapidly rising to power. The prophet perceived in him an agent of the Lord to overthrow the Babylonians and free the Jews from captivity:

> Thus saith Jehovah, thy Redeemer . . . I am Jehovah, that maketh all things; that stretcheth forth the heavens alone; that spreadeth abroad the earth . . . that saith of Jerusalem, She shall be inhabited; and of the cities of Judah, They shall be built . . . that saith of Cyrus, *He is* my shepherd, and shall perform all my pleasure, even saying of Jerusalem, She shall be built; and of the temple, Thy foundation shall be laid (Isa. 44:24-28).

Chapters 49-55 of The Book of Isaiah deal primarily with the Servant of Jehovah (the Christ) and describe the glory that shall be Jerusalem's. There are four passages relating to the Servant: 42:1-7; 49:1-6; 50:4-9; and 52:13 to 53:12. These are poems or songs, the first of which describes the Servant in whom the Lord delights and who shall bring forth judgment. The second announces the Servant's understanding of His divine mission to both Jew and Gentile (for the mission of the Servant is world-wide). The third song states that the Servant shall receive wisdom of the Lord and, even though persecuted, will have faith and remain steadfast. The fourth and longest song provides the clearest picture of the Servant. Deprived of health, possessions, and reputation, He shall be misunderstood and dishonored. Nevertheless, He will endure His suffering without complaint, that many may be saved. "He shall bear their iniquities" (Isa. 53:11). Finally, however, comes the note of triumph, "Behold, my servant shall deal wisely, he shall be exalted and lifted up, and shall be very high" (Isa. 52:13).

The idea of vicarious suffering—that is, one person suffering for the sins of others—here presented by Deutero-Isaiah, was new to Jewish thought. The Jews believed suffering to be the result of sin, but this prophet presented the conception that an innocent one may suffer voluntarily in order to bring others to a realization of their wrongdoing and induce penitence and subsequent redemption. Such belief has, of course, been prominent in Christian theology.

There have been many divergent opinions as to the identity of the Servant of Jehovah. Jeremiah, Zerubbabel, and even Deutero-Isaiah have been so designated, especially by Jewish scholars. Christians generally see in these songs a description of Jesus Christ. The consensus among Bible authorities is that Israel, the nation in a Messianic role, is meant. As a nation Israel failed to achieve the service predicted for the Servant, and it found fulfillment only in the work of Jesus Christ. Deutero-Isaiah conceived of one who would conquer the sins of humanity through love and obedience to the Highest, and surely Jesus Christ proved the validity of the great prophet's ideal.

There is still a more profound interpretation of the Servant, which is revealed in our study of Truth. Man's divine self, the Christ indwelling, is the potential Servant of Jehovah. When we function in the mortal consciousness the Servant is shunned and abused but remains faithful awaiting our recognition. As we unfold spiritually, the Servant rises triumphant in consciousness. Man in his fully redeemed state is the active Servant of Jehovah, actuated by love in his service to others and filled with power to speak the Truth that alone can make men free.

Deutero-Isaiah ends his prophetic messages by depicting the future glory of Jerusalem—which, however, shall be dependent upon the people's responsiveness to God. He cries to them in the name of Jehovah: "Incline your ear, and come unto me; hear, and your soul shall live" (Isa. 55:3). Then theirs shall be the glorious task of witnessing for the Lord.

Surely this great unknown prophet was unconsciously describing himself when he declared:

"How beautiful upon the mountains are the feet of him that bringeth good tidings, that publisheth peace . . . that saith unto Zion, Thy God reigneth!" (Isa. 52:7).

CHAPTER XVI

The Restoration

Part I

Ezra 1-6; Haggai; Zechariah; Isaiah (56-66);
Obadiah; Malachi

THE PERSIAN KING Cyrus proved to be a wise and just sovereign. Many peoples were transplanted within his vast empire, and he gave them permission to return to their native lands subject to the overlordship of Persia. Among those who benefited by this were the Jews. Not only did Cyrus allow them to return to Jerusalem but he gave back the Temple vessels that Nebuchadnezzar had brought to Babylon.

The great day of release was at hand, yet only a comparatively small number of Jews took advantage of it. The ones who had been transported from Judah in 597 B.C. were too old, generally; those who had been in Babylonia since 586 B.C., and the Jews who had been born in Babylonia were accustomed to the country and did not want to leave. The prophets of the eighth and seventh centuries B.C. had foreseen that a remnant would return, and it was indeed the spiritual-minded to whom Jehovah and the Holy City were of paramount importance. Only they were willing to undertake the long journey to Judah and establish a new life.

Always the search for the things of the Spirit is

a courageous adventure into the unknown, but those who love the Lord put Him first. The Jews who remained in Babylonia gave moral and financial support to the intrepid group whose high hopes were to rebuild Jerusalem and the Temple. It is much easier to give such support than to give of ourselves. We will gladly support a religious enterprise with funds but we are reluctant to give our hearts to God. Only when we are quickened to the realization that the more abundant life is to be found in a harmonious relationship with God will we willingly surrender the things of the world for the priceless treasures of the kingdom.

Sheshbazzar was in charge of the company of returning Jews, though the two names most prominently connected with the activities of the group are Zerubbabel and Jeshua (often call Joshua by Bible students). Whether Sheshbazzar was the uncle of Zerubbabel, as some Bible authorities believe, or whether he was a Persian officer appointed by Cyrus, is uncertain. In any event, Zerubbabel succeeded Sheshbazzar as leader, and the events of this period, as recorded in The Book of Ezra, deal primarily with Zerubbabel and Jeshua.

Zerubbabel was a member of the house of David, the grandson of Jehoiachin. Zerubbabel signifies:

A very strong and influential thought activity belonging to the spiritual phase of man. . . . This spiritual thought activity becomes a leading factor in putting away error illusions and restoring the worship of God, with its resultant good (M.D. 697).

Jeshua was of the priestly line and served as high priest. He represents "salvation or redemption through Jehovah, I AM" (M.D. 345).

These two, Zerubbabel and Jeshua, working together emphasize the value of spiritual consciousness in re-establishing a community, or a life, on the right basis.

The period of the restoration symbolizes our return to Spirit and our efforts to sustain a spiritual consciousness. During a time of trial (exile) we turn to God and our release eventually comes. However, it is one thing to gain a spiritual blessing, such as freedom, but quite another thing to maintain it. The people who returned to Jerusalem loved their God sufficiently to desire to rebuild His city and His Temple, even as we willingly give of ourselves to a righteous undertaking. We start with devotion and zeal, but it is not easy to keep at our task in the face of trials. In the experiences of the Jews we find some of our own hardships duplicated, and from their great teachers and leaders come the lessons necessary to us.

The party found Jerusalem in ruins. The poorer class of Jews who had been left behind when Nebuchadnezzar destroyed the city had made no effort to restore the Temple or the city. The newcomers were immediately confronted with the serious problem of laying the foundation of an adequate economic existence as well as establishing a religious life. They knew that it was all-important to have some place of worship, and a rough stone altar was set up on

Mount Zion; there burnt offerings were made, the regular morning and evening oblations resumed, and feast days observed. As soon as possible timber was bought from the Phoenicians and masons and carpenters were engaged to begin the Temple.

The surrounding peoples resented the return of the Jews and warred on them, giving them no peace. When this hostility did not succeed, a group of Samaritans offered assistance in the construction of the Temple, but Zerubbabel and Jeshua said:

> Ye have nothing to do with us in building a house unto our God; but we ourselves together will build unto Jehovah, the God of Israel, as king Cyrus the king of Persia hath commanded us (Ezra 4:3).

The Samaritans, whose homeland was north of Judah, were a mixed race, the descendants of the Israelites left in the country when the northern kingdom of Israel fell to the Assyrians in 722 B.C., and of colonists imported into the land. The Judean Jews would have no dealings with them. Even in the time of Jesus they still considered the Samaritans inferior racially and religiously. The spiritual idea involved is that we cannot build a spiritual consciousness (temple) with a divided mind and heart. The Samaritans represent "mixed thoughts, partly worldly and partly religious. . . . a state of consciousness in which Truth and error are mixed" (M.D. 568). Spiritual development demands a complete separation between the true and the false. Our temple can be constructed by spiritual thought only. The

Jewish leaders represent one established in spiritual consciousness who wisely rejects what is offered by the sense mind.

In retaliation for the Jews' refusal to let them help with the Temple, the Samaritans "weakened the hands of the people of Judah, and troubled them in building, and hired counsellors against them, to frustrate their purpose" (Ezra 4:4, 5). They even wrote a letter to the Persian king accusing the Jews of strengthening their position in order to resist Persian rule. These hindrances so discouraged the Jews that they stopped work on the Temple and sank into an apathetic frame of mind. Here again the spiritual was cast aside by mortal thought.

However, when we have once started on the spiritual path the Lord does not permit us to drift too far, and in time the spiritual idea reasserts itself. Historically, the prophets Haggai and Zechariah were the ones who aroused the Jews to a sense of the necessity of completing the house of Jehovah, sixteen years after work on it had been begun and a few years after it had been discontinued.

Haggai (520 B.C.)

Very little is known of this prophet. It is thought that he was among the Jews taken into captivity in 586 B.C. and that he accompanied Zerubbabel and Jeshua to Jerusalem. If this is so, Haggai was quite elderly when in 520 B.C. he gave his messages urging his countrymen to complete the Temple.

Haggai realized that without the visible presence

of a house consecrated to the Lord the masses would
not have the spiritual impetus to obey His will, and
upon that impetus depended their well-being. They
were giving their entire time and attention to crops,
business, and other material interests. Just prior to
Haggai's opening message a severe drought had
caused a poor harvest. It seemed to the people that
though they worked diligently their labor was to no
avail. Haggai contended that so long as they neg-
lected their religious duty—failed to complete the
Temple—their efforts could not produce good results:

Is it a time for you yourselves to dwell in your ceiled
houses, while this house [the Temple] lieth waste? Now
therefore thus saith Jehovah of hosts: Consider your ways.
Ye have sown much, and bring in little; ye eat, but ye
have not enough; ye drink, but ye are not filled with drink;
ye clothe you, but there is none warm; and he that earneth
wages earneth wages *to put it* into a bag with holes (Hag.
1:4-6).

No life can be truly successful unless it is founded
on spiritual Principle. Temptations come to all of us
to neglect the spiritual side of life. We can easily
drift into the rut of material interests, quite forgetting that the outer can never change for the better
until there is a renewal of the consciousness. The
longer we stay away from the Lord the harder it is
to get back to Him, and we need to assert the strong
spiritual thought represented by Haggai. This brings
to our attention the necessity of co-operating with
God (building the Temple). Haggai clearly saw

the futility of working without God. We indeed "have sown much, and bring in little," we earn wages only *"to put it* into a bag with holes" (Hag. 1:6).

Charles Fillmore states that Haggai represents:

A realization of good as taking the place of seeming evil. That spiritual insight in man which heralds joyous, full, free deliverance from oppression, and abundance of rich substance and life for mind and body; it feasts upon the Truth daily, and foresees and foretells the working out of good (M.D. 248).

At the time Haggai addressed his people, Darius I (who came to be called Darius the Great) had recently ascended the throne of Persia. King Cyrus, who had given the Jews permission to return to Jerusalem in 537 B.C., died in 528 B.C., and was succeeded by his son Cambyses. Cambyses conquered Egypt and made the Persian empire the greatest in territorial extent the world had yet known. However, he did not have the wisdom of his father in the management of the vast domain, and dissension was rife. While the king was at war, a pretender seized the throne, and Cambyses died or committed suicide. After a few months the usurper was slain by a group of nobles, who selected one of their own number, Darius, as sovereign. As Darius was not the rightful heir, the beginning of his rule was marked by revolts on every side. These conditions were spoken of by both Haggai and his contemporary, Zechariah. The political upheavals apparently aroused the prophets of Judah to a sense of sudden opportunity

and possible freedom. Judah's immediate task was
to rebuild the Temple and deserve divine favor. So
Haggai urged:

> Go up to the mountain, and bring wood, and build
> the house; and I will take pleasure in it, and I will be
> glorified, saith Jehovah (Hag. 1:8).

Haggai, who probably had seen Solomon's
Temple, which was a most imposing building, knew
that it could not then be duplicated in splendor. He
therefore warned the people against disappointment
in the new Temple: promising that Jehovah would
glorify it and "The latter glory of this house shall be
greater than the former . . . and in this place will I
[Jehovah] give peace" (Hag. 2:9).

Zechariah (520-518 B.C.)

Zechariah began his prophetic work in the same
year as Haggai and continued for several years
longer. While he was as insistent as Haggai in the
matter of completion of the Temple, the greater
part of his messages consists of a series of visions
describing the blessings of the coming spiritual age.
His book is in two parts, chapters 1-8 and chapters
9-14. The messages contained in the first eight chapters are known to have been given by Zechariah,
but it is thought that the remaining chapters belong
to a later period and were inserted into Zechariah's
work. They form part of the apocalyptic literature
of the Bible.

Zechariah signifies "spiritual consciousness . . .
or the entrance of spiritual thought into man's con-

sciousness and a lifting up of spiritual understanding" (M.D. 684). When this quality is foremost in mind, we are confident that all will be well as we put our trust in Jehovah. Though Zechariah knew he was addressing a disappointed and discouraged people, he cried:

And it shall come to pass that, as ye were a curse among the nations, O house of Judah and house of Israel, so will I save you, and ye shall be a blessing. Fear not, but let your hands be strong. For thus saith Jehovah of hosts: As I thought to do evil unto you, when your fathers provoked me to wrath . . . and I repented not; so again have I thought in these days to do good unto Jerusalem and to the house of Judah: fear ye not (Zech. 8:13-15).

When we are disobedient to God's law it seems as if we are cursed, in that hardships of all kinds overtake us. But when we turn again to Him, a blessing is forthcoming. To eliminate fear from the mind and be strong in faith and works is the course before us.

Like his great predecessors, Zechariah was convinced that a high moral and ethical standard was required:

These are the things that ye shall do: Speak ye every man the truth with his neighbor; execute the judgment of truth and peace in your gates; and let none of you devise evil in your hearts against his neighbor; and love no false oath: for all these are things that I hate, saith Jehovah (Zech. 8:16, 17).

Zechariah delighted in telling of the security his people would feel with Jehovah as their protector.

Jerusalem would not need outer defenses: "For I, saith Jehovah, will be unto her a wall of fire round about, and I will be the glory in the midst of her" (Zech. 2:5).

According to Zechariah's prediction, Zerubbabel of the royal line of David was to be the political leader of the new age for the Jews, and Jeshua the religious leader. This prophecy was not fulfilled in an outer sense, but prophecy invariably finds fulfillment when considered spiritually. The new age for man is ever ushered in when spiritual ideas, such as typified by Zerubbabel and Jeshua, dominate his mind. The change for the better could not come by physical force, said Zechariah. "Not by might, nor by power, but by my Spirit, saith Jehovah of hosts" (Zech. 4:6).

How well for us to remember this! It is only by the infiltration of spiritual thoughts and feelings into consciousness that opposing forces in the outer (human problems) are overcome. Our good is brought into manifestation by the power of His Spirit working mightily in us.

In a spirit of joyous expectancy Zechariah exclaimed,

Sing and rejoice, O daughter of Zion; for, lo, I come, and I will dwell in the midst of thee, saith Jehovah (Zech. 2:10).

The messages of Haggai and Zechariah so aroused the Jews that they set to work in earnest, and the Temple was completed within a period of four years. It was dedicated in 516 B.C. with the celebration of the Passover.

Jewish hopes of freedom as the result of Persia's difficulties were not realized, but there was peace in the little land of Judah. The Persian kings were not hard overlords and, despite various internal problems that arose among the Jews, the Temple proved to be a rallying factor not only in Palestine but throughout the Mediterranean world wherever the Jews lived. Three prophets spoke in Jerusalem during the half century following the completion of the Temple, III Isaiah or Trito-Isaiah, Obadiah, and Malachi.

Trito-Isaiah (early part of fifth century)
Isaiah 56-66

More in the spirit of I Isaiah than of Deutero-Isaiah, Trito-Isaiah berated the people soundly for the religious evils still in existence, especially the neglect of the Sabbath. He also called them to task for immorality and irreligious conduct, which he was convinced was due to the failure of Jewish leaders and priests to uphold high ideals. He made splendid promises in the name of Jehovah to the righteous, but declared that "the wicked are like the troubled sea; for it cannot rest, and its waters cast up mire and dirt. There is no peace, saith my God, to the wicked" (Isa. 57:20, 21).

The prophet denounced formal fasting, which had always been a part of religious observance but had been practiced to excess during the Exile and following it:

Is such the fast that I have chosen? the day for a man
to afflict his soul? Is it to bow down his head as a rush,
and to spread sackcloth and ashes under him? wilt thou
call this a fast, and an acceptable day to Jehovah? (Isa.
58:5).

Always these enlightened prophets denounced
outer devotional acts that were without a corresponding inner reformation. Fasting should not be a mere
refraining from food nor repentance in sackcloth.
Spiritually considered, fasting is a refraining from
destructive thoughts, feelings, and deeds, and sub-
stituting spiritual action therefor. Trito-Isaiah described the true fast:

Is not this the fast that I have chosen: to loose the
bonds of wickedness, to undo the bands of the yoke, and
to let the oppressed go free, and that ye break every yoke?
Is it not to deal thy bread to the hungry, and that thou
bring the poor that are cast out of thy house? when thou
seest the naked, that thou cover him; and that thou hide
not thyself from thine own flesh? (Isa. 58:6, 7).

As we reject the false and accept the true, we
practice a spiritual fast that is most acceptable to the
Lord, and the prophet declares:

Then shall thy light break forth as the morning, and
thy healing shall spring forth speedily; and thy righteousness shall go before thee . . . Then shalt thou call, and
Jehovah will answer; thou shalt cry, and he will say,
Here I am (Isa. 58:8, 9).

Trito-Isaiah's inspiring words, "Arise, shine; for
thy light is come, and the glory of Jehovah is risen
upon thee" (Isa. 60:1), must have lifted the hearts
of his people as they lift ours today. We can rise in

consciousness; when we do, the radiant life of Spirit shines through us to bring true peace and wholeness:

For, behold, I create new heavens and a new earth; and the former things shall not be remembered, nor come into mind. But be ye glad and rejoice for ever in that which I create; for, behold, I create Jerusalem a rejoicing, and her people a joy. . . . And it shall come to pass that, before they call, I will answer; and while they are yet speaking, I will hear (Isa. 65:17, 18, 24).

Obadiah (500-450 B.C.)

Obadiah gave his messages sometime between the completion of the Temple and the coming of Ezra to Jerusalem. They consist of denunciations of Edom and predictions of her doom. Edom was the country to the south of Judah and had been the Jews' enemy for centuries. The Edomites were descendants of Esau, the one who sold his birthright for a mess of pottage, while the Jews were the descendants of Jacob, the one who received the name Israel. The former were wholly materialistic in their outlook and, jealous of the Jews, rejoiced when their country fell in 586 B.C. Edom took every advantage of Judah's misfortune and for this gained the hatred of the Jews.

The Book of Obadiah is the shortest in the Old Testament, consisting of only one chapter.

Charles Fillmore states that Obadiah represents:

The higher thoughts in man that serve and worship God through the I AM, Jehovah, indwelling Christ. They are faithful and true. They are thoughts that are obedient to spiritual ideals, that hear and heed the voice of Spirit (M.D. 489).

There are two passages in The Book of Obadiah that are especially worthy of remembering. The first is a prediction of Edom's downfall:

Though thou mount on high as the eagle, and though thy nest be set among the stars, I will bring thee down from thence, saith Jehovah (Obad. 1:4).

When the higher thoughts become active in consciousness, we realize that no matter how mighty we become when dominated by Edom (sense consciousness), the law of the Lord shall bring us down. This is ever the fate of man functioning apart from God.

The second outstanding passage in Obadiah's book relates the inevitable reward of a spiritual attitude:

But in Mount Zion there shall be those that escape, and it shall be holy; and the house of Jacob shall possess their possessions (Obad. 1:17).

As we learn to harmonize ourselves with our indwelling Lord, we escape the evils that attend persons who live in sense consciousness; we experience holiness or wholeness. In the house of Jacob (spiritual consciousness) we shall possess our possessions instead of our possessions possessing us.

Malachi (460-444 B.C.)

The prophet whose messages constitute the last book of the Old Testament is unknown by name. Malachi means "servant," or "messenger of Jehovah" (M.D. 420), and nowhere in the book is a specific name given. He told his countrymen that the Lord's seeming indifference to them was due to their indifference to Him. When we receive no help from God it is because of our neglect of Him. God can do for us only what He can do through us, and if we fail to open ourselves to His good, it appears that He has forsaken us.

Malachi criticized the priests and the entire religious system and rebuked the people for laxity in morals. He declared that a day of judgment was coming soon in which the wicked would be punished. His condemnation of the Jews for their failure to pay the Temple dues is perhaps the most familiar passage in his book:

> Return unto me, and I will return unto you saith Jehovah of hosts. But ye say, Wherein shall we return? Will a man rob God? yet ye rob me. But ye say, Wherein have we robbed thee? In tithes and offerings. . . . Bring ye the whole tithe into the store-house, that there may be food in my house, and prove me now herewith, saith Jehovah of hosts, if I will not open you the windows of heaven, and pour you out a blessing, that there shall not be room enough *to receive it* (Mal. 3:7-10).

The prophet assured the righteous that they would not be forgotten in the Day of Judgment:

> They shall be mine, saith Jehovah of hosts, *even* mine own possession, in the day that I make; and I will spare them, as a man spareth his own son that serveth him (Mal. 3:17).

Charles Fillmore states that Malachi represents "the voice of conscience in man," which "calls his at-

tention to his shortcomings and encourages him to
turn to God and do right." He adds the following:

All real lasting wealth and happiness are based on unity
with God. Malachi will tell you this, or you can prove it
for yourself after you have spent years in material experiences (M.D. 420).

CHAPTER XVII

The Restoration

Part II
Ezra 7-10; Nehemiah

AT THE BEGINNING of the fifth century B.C. the Greeks were slowly rising to power, and Darius of Persia was determined to subdue them. When, however, the Persian force met the Athenians at Marathon, it was defeated. In the midst of preparation for another expedition against Greece, Darius died. His son Xerxes I continued the father's plans. At the battles of Salamis (480 B.C.) and Plataea (479 B.C.), the huge fleet and army of Persia were routed. The Greeks became aggressive, and throughout the next century the power of Persia gradually declined.

Artaxerxes I came to the throne of Persia in 465 B.C., and reigned until 424 B.C. During those years two outstanding leaders of the Jews did their work.

Though the building of the second Temple in Jerusalem (called Zerubbabel's Temple) was of benefit to Jewish prestige, the conditions in Judah generally were far from satisfactory. Jerusalem's walls were still in ruins, and the city was at the mercy of marauding tribes. It was also scantily populated, and most of the inhabitants were poor. Many social and economic evils existed. On the other hand, the Jews who had remained in Babylonia were living peaceably, and some had accumulated wealth and

obtained positions of influence. Naturally they knew
something of the hardships of their kinsmen in
Judah, and when a small deputation of Jews came
from Judah seeking help, Ezra, and later Nehemiah
—two outstanding Jews—responded to the call. Each
of these men left memoirs of his own deeds and
works, and these now form the books of Ezra and
Nehemiah.

In 458 B.C. Ezra secured a royal decree permitting him to visit Jerusalem. Gathering a company of
some fifteen hundred, Ezra left Persia bearing rich
gifts to the Temple, not only from the Jews in Babylonia but even from Artaxerxes I.

Ezra was a scribe and an earnest student of the
law. Among the Jews in Babylonia there had risen
the priestly school of writers whose great achieve-
ment was the formulation of an elaborate code of religious practices to govern almost every act of every-
day life. Those who interpreted and expounded the
law were known as scribes. Ezra is commonly referred to as the "father of the scribes."

When Ezra arrived in Jerusalem he had the
Priestly Code with him and intended to introduce it
for use in the Temple to take the place of the less
stringent regulations contained in Deuteronomy,
which the Judean Jews were following. He was positive that the more elaborate and exacting ritual
would be beneficial to the Temple service and tend
to stimulate individual piety. The Jews had grown
lax in religious observance, and many evils were
prevalent. Those to which Ezra objected most were

intermarriage with Gentiles (people of surrounding
nations, such as Ammonites, Moabites, Samaritans),
indiscriminate divorce, and indifference in keeping
the laws of the Sabbath. Ezra's first move was against
intermarriage, and he was so vigorously opposed that
for the time being he set aside his main project, the
introduction of the Priestly Code.

We find in the man Ezra the thought of the spirit
of loyalty to Truth: "For Ezra had set his heart to seek
the law of Jehovah, and to do it" (Ezra 7:10). Ezra is often
called the Puritan of the Bible. Metaphysically, therefore,
he represents order, the faculty of the mind that holds
every thought and act strictly to the Truth of Being, regardless of circumstances or environments (M.D. 213).

The underlying purpose of the Priestly Code was
to establish order and intensify religious zeal. In our
own ongoing we need just what this code was designed to accomplish.

Order is truly "heaven's first law," and if we are
to grow spiritually we need to establish system in
our religious life. To have daily periods for study
and prayer is advisable. When outer interests or du-
ties are pressing, it is often a temptation to post-
pone prayer. However, if the faculty of order (typified by Ezra) is prominent in consciousness we shall
let nothing interfere with those precious moments
of communion with God. What we are in consciousness is much more important than what we do. Judging from the human viewpoint, physical and mental
accomplishment is the goal, but as we progress along
spiritual lines we commence to realize that the im-

portant business before us is to keep our contact with
the Lord steady and sure. Then our outer affairs will
be in order and successful. But to keep the vital inner
contact with God demands regular times of seeking
His Spirit indwelling. This requires discipline, and
discipline is a word the human self does not like.
Exacting teachers like Ezra are never popular, but
they play an important part in our development,
and in time we rise to call them blessed.

Judaism was so strengthened by what Ezra did
for the Jews that it successfully resisted pagan
thought in the next century. Order and loyalty to
Truth safeguard our consciousness against the destructive forces that are prevalent in a materialistic
society.

Other changes had to take place before the people were willing to listen to Ezra, and these were
brought about by Nehemiah, one of the most color-
ful and dynamic leaders the Jews ever had.

We make our first acquaintance with Nehemiah
at the court of the Persian king Artaxerxes I. There
Nehemiah held a position of power, being "cup bear-
er to the king" (Neh. 2:1), which probably meant a
minister of state. A committee of Jews came to Persia seeking Nehemiah's assistance. When Nehemiah
heard of the distress of his people, he was overwhelmed. "I sat down and wept," he relates, "and
mourned certain days; and I fasted and prayed before the God of heaven" (Neh. 1:4).

It was Nehemiah's ardent desire to go to the
Holy City and help his people, but he could not make

such a journey without the king's consent. After several months a propitious time came to present his request. One day as Nehemiah handed wine to him, Artaxerxes asked, "Why is thy countenance sad, seeing thou art not sick? this is nothing else but sorrow of heart" (Neh. 2:2). For a moment Nehemiah was "very sore afraid," for much depended on how he answered. Perhaps he recalled Jehovah's promise to Moses, "I will be with thy mouth, and teach thee what thou shalt speak" (Exod. 4:12), and leaned upon it. In any event, Nehemiah presented his case well, and King Artaxerxes gave him permission to go to Jerusalem. He also provided Nehemiah with letters to the Persian governor that stated that Nehemiah was to rebuild the walls of Jerusalem. An order for supplies and an armed escort were likewise furnished. When our motive is right—that is, when our desire is to serve unselfishly—God prepares our way, often through a human agency.

Nehemiah signifies "that in us which inspires us to higher and better things. He represents, too, the boldness and the courage that set about the rebuilding of a character weakened by sin" (M.D. 476).

Before we are ready to accept the recommendations of Ezra, we must do some preliminary work. The Nehemiah state of consciousness has to rebuild the walls of Jerusalem. Jerusalem represents the consciousness of peace that is protected by spiritual thoughts (walls). If these walls have been destroyed (that is, if our spiritual consciousness has been overthrown by adverse thoughts), reconstruction is necessary. However, it is not always easy. When we have lived in limiting conditions and accepted them as inevitable, only the inspiration and courage represented by Nehemiah will enable us to rebuild a spiritual consciousness. Those who have once been aware of the divine presence and have lost that awareness understand the great necessity for regaining it.

Upon arriving in Jerusalem, Nehemiah conferred with the leaders. One night he went out alone to look the situation over:

> Then went I up in the night by the brook, and viewed the wall; and I turned back, and entered by the valley gate, and returned. And the rulers knew not whither I went, or what I did; neither had I as yet told it to the Jews, nor to the priests, nor to the nobles, nor to the rulers, nor to the rest that did the work (Neh. 2:15, 16).

Is it not best to work out a plan with God before we ask outer help? Many a worthy endeavor fails because we talk about it too much beforehand, seeking advice here, there, and everywhere. Much discussion dissipates the energy required to perform the deed!

With a course of action in mind, Nehemiah then talked to the people:

> I told them of the hand of my God which was good upon me, as also of the king's words that he had spoken unto me. And they said, Let us rise up and build. So they strengthened their hands for the good *work* (Neh. 2:18).

Nehemiah's capable and aggressive leadership aroused a new national spirit, and Jews came from

Jericho, Tekoa, Gibeon, and Mizpah to assist in building the walls.

A plan conceived by divine direction goes forward, but there are often hindrances of various sorts. Some arose for Nehemiah. Sanballat the Horonite, Tobiah the Ammonite, and Geshem the Arabian attempted to stop the building project. Each of these represents a phase of the sense mind that is quite apt to interfere with the rebuilding of a spiritual consciousness. Sanballat signifies "error thoughts and fears of which we have not as yet really become conscious, but which are working with seemingly great strength in our subconsciousness" (M.D. 572). Tobiah the Ammonite represents "a wild, uncultivated state of consciousness, which thoughts of sensuality, sin, and ignorance have formed in the outer, worldly phase of man's being" (M.D. 661). Geshem the Arabian signifies "unproductive thoughts and tendencies," especially "the permanent materiality of man's outer consciousness and body" (M.D. 224).

Everyone who attempts to advance spiritually has to contend with unredeemed thoughts and emotions. Nehemiah's motive was misconstrued, and he was accused by his enemies of strengthening Jerusalem in order to rebel against the Persian king. Nehemiah states:

> Then answered I them, and said unto them, The God of heaven, he will prosper us; therefore we his servants will arise and build; but ye have no portion, nor right, nor memorial, in Jerusalem (Neh. 2:20).

Thus repulsed, Tobiah tried ridicule, saying, "Even that which they are building, if a fox go up, he shall break down their stone wall" (Neh. 4:3). Nehemiah answered this by prayer. Sanballat then gathered a force to attack the Jews. Nehemiah was compelled to organize two divisions of workmen, one to build and another to defend the builders. In writing of the caution and persistence with which the work was carried on, Nehemiah naïvely records,

So neither I, nor my brethren, nor my servants, nor the men of the guard that followed me, none of us put off our clothes, every one *went with* his weapon *to* the water (Neh. 4:23).

Unceasing vigilance is the price of success along any line.

Despite all forms of opposition the walls of Jerusalem were completed "in fifty and two days" (Neh. 6:15). The work was completed in Elul (September) 444 B.C. Jerusalem's population was soon greatly increased by those moving into the city from small surrounding towns. This made for greater prosperity. Also Nehemiah appointed a special governor, Hanani, to be in charge of the city, to make sure that its affairs were properly administered.

Nehemiah had been appointed governor of the province by the Persian king, and when the walls were completed he promptly turned his attention to much-needed reforms. The well-to-do were preying mercilessly upon the helpless and needy, exacting usury and charging exorbitant prices for food and land. Nehemiah summoned the people to a great council and denounced "the nobles and the rulers" (Neh. 5:7) unsparingly. He was able to point to his own generous example of unselfishness, telling them that, as he was governor, he and his servants could have received upkeep from taxes as the former governors had done, but that throughout his stay and even when the walls were being built, he had met the expenses of his own household, besides entertaining many Jews and rulers. "Yet for all this I demanded not the bread of the governor, because the bondage was heavy upon this people" (Neh. 5:18). He concluded these remarks with his characteristic prayer, in which may we be worthy to join: "Remember unto me, O my God, for good, all that I have done for this people" (Neh. 5:19).

Actions invariably speak louder than words. To make a plea for generosity without practicing it is often without avail, but the plea is effective when sustained by deeds. The people promptly agreed to the reforms proposed by Nehemiah.

With the populace in a happier frame of mind, it was the psychological moment for Ezra to introduce religious reforms, principally adoption of the Priestly Code as a model for worship. An assembly was called and "all the people were *attentive* unto the book of the law" (Neh. 8:3). For seven days Ezra read to them. His listeners were much impressed, very penitent, and willingly observed the Feast of Tabernacles as bidden. They also signed a covenant to obey four specific provisions outlined by Ezra: (1) abstention from marriage with Gentiles,

(2) proper observance of the Sabbath, (3) observance of the sabbatical year, (4) regular and responsible support of the Temple and its ministry.

These were helpful though firm provisions. When considered spiritually each has an important bearing on our own spiritual life. The first carries the idea that we are not to adulterate pure spiritual ideas with nonspiritual concepts. In the Bible, when metaphysically considered, the Jews represent the spiritual mind while the Gentiles stand for phases of the sense mind. To mix the two leads to a "house [consciousness] divided against itself" (Matt. 12:25). Paul brings out the same thought in writing the Corinthians: "Be not unequally yoked with unbelievers: for what fellowship have righteousness and iniquity? and what communion hath light with darkness?" (II Cor. 6:14). Our consciousness should be sustained on the highest spiritual level.

The rule governing observance of the Sabbath is also vital to us. The true Sabbath occurs when we rest in the Lord, and refers to our time of prayer when strength is renewed and the mind responsive to divine ideas.

The third provision, observance of the sabbatical year, required that the people let their lands lie fallow every seventh year; also that they remit the debt of a fellow Jew at the seventh year. Seven is the Hebrew number of completion. Charles Fillmore states that the number seven represents "fullness in the world of phenomena; seven always refers to the divine law of perfection for the divine-natural man"

(M.D. 585). Therefore, to release the land every seventh year implies fulfilling the divine or natural law of our being. To remit the debts of a fellow man is compliance with the spiritual law of forgiveness.

The fourth stipulation, support of the Temple and its ministry, has both an outer and an inner significance. It is our reasonable service to contribute to the religious organization to which we belong. Also, it is our reasonable service to support the inner temple of Truth by contributing the substance of our pure thought, which is worship, and to sustain it by right action.

Nehemiah was recalled to Persia sometime after Ezra had instituted his reforms, and during his absence old abuses reappeared. The Temple precincts were profaned, the priests did not receive their lawful dues, the Sabbath laws were broken, and intermarriage with other races began again. It looked as if the labors of the two reformers were unavailing. Happily, Nehemiah returned to Jerusalem in 432 B.C., and these evils received prompt attention and correction.

Tobiah the Ammonite had been occupying a room within the Temple. Not only was this space needed for storing tithes, but it was unlawful for a Gentile to live in the Temple. As recorded in an earlier portion of this lesson, Tobiah represents an unregenerate state of consciousness. This must be cast out completely with all its belongings. Tobiah's quarters were then cleaned thoroughly and made a fit place for the storage of tithes (spiritual use).

What Tobiah represents is quite likely to usurp a place in our consciousness. Have we the Nehemiah courage to cast him out, bag and baggage, and preserve the sanctity of the premises of our being?

Nehemiah also insisted upon the proper observance of the Sabbath, and enforced the rule pertaining to intermarriage. The grandson of the high priest had married the daughter of Sanballat the Horonite, who with Tobiah had caused Nehemiah great difficulty when the walls of Jerusalem were being built. The couple was expelled with dispatch.

Viewed historically, these great leaders, Nehemiah and Ezra, established the community on a sound basis and strengthened Judaism. Viewed spiritually, Nehemiah (courage) and Ezra (order), working together, lift the consciousness to a level of spiritual activity and make for harmony and prosperity in affairs.

CHAPTER XVIII

Intertestamental Period

Part I
Ruth; Jonah; Joel; Ecclesiastes

A PERIOD of some four centuries lay between the time of Ezra and Nehemiah and the beginning of the Christian Era. Hebrew history, as recorded in the Bible, ends with the reforms of these two men. It is from secular history, principally the Jewish historian Josephus, that a knowledge of the events of this long period is gained. The Apocryphal books of I and II Maccabees also give valuable historical data. These centuries were a time of great literary activity for the Jews and a number of the canonical books were produced. This and the following chapter will give a brief outline of the main events and the Unity interpretation of the books of the Old Testament written during this period.

Judea, as the country of Judah is referred to in later Hebrew history and New Testament times (Judea is the Greco-Roman equivalent of Judah), remained a province of the Persian empire until 333 B.C. The rule of Persia was not harsh. There seemed to be no way for the Jews to gain political independence, so they centered their attention on the development of religion. The effect of Ezra's reforms was to intensify interest in religion and its practices, and the Temple, under the administration of the high priest, became the center of life and worship. The law and the ritual, with perfect obedience thereto, were the chief concern of the Jew.

The highly organized form of religion preserved Judaism and was of great benefit in that sense, but it tended to develop narrowness, exclusiveness, and self-righteousness on the part of its adherents. As a protest against the extreme orthodox system established by Ezra and added to by subsequent teachers of Judaism, the books of Ruth and Jonah were written.

The Book of Ruth (written about 400 B.C.)

Ezra had been firm in his conviction that there should be no intermarriage between Jew and Gentile. The Book of Ruth purports to show that a mixed marriage can prove to be highly beneficial. Ruth, a Moabitess, accepts Judaism, is wed to a Jew, and enriches the race, becoming an ancestress of David, Israel's greatest king. The book may contain some historical material, though its main object was to emphasize the fact that it is the individual, not the nationality, that counts.

The scene of Ruth is laid in an ancient period, "in the days when the judges judged" (Ruth 1:1), the time immediately following the conquest of Canaan. Its spiritual interpretation is rich indeed. Naomi, a Jewess, represents one who has a knowledge of spiritual things but in time of distress (famine) leaves Bethlehem (spiritual substance) and goes with her husband and two sons to Moab (a lower or more material state of mind). There she encounters hardship. Her husband dies, and her two sons, who marry women of the country, also die. Whenever we revert to the material because it seems difficult to work out our problems with God's help, the result is always disastrous.

Bereft of her family, Naomi decides to return to Bethlehem. She feels forsaken and alone. Her two daughters-in-law Orpah and Ruth offer to accompany her, but she bids them turn again to their own land. Orpah follows her advice, but Ruth cleaves to her.

Orpah represents "a youthfulness, grace, and activity in the natural soul . . . and zeal, but more for the things of self than the things of Spirit" (M.D. 497). This side of our consciousness, while it may have some affection for the spiritual, finds its real interest in the outer world and willingly returns thereto.

Ruth represents "the love of the natural soul for God and for the things of Spirit. Ruth is a type of the beautiful, the pure, and the loving characteristics of the natural man" (M.D. 562). When this phase of consciousness comes in contact with the spiritual (Naomi), it holds tenaciously to it. Ruth will not hear of returning to Moab. When we read the beautiful words Ruth spoke to Naomi they become increasingly meaningful, for they signify the desire of the awakened soul to hold fast to the highest:

Entreat me not to leave thee, or to return from following after thee, for whither thou goest, I will go; and where thou lodgest, I will lodge; thy people shall be my

people, and thy God my God, where thou diest, will I
die, and there will I be buried: Jehovah do so to me, and
more also, if aught but death part thee and me (Ruth
1:16, 17).

Naomi has a wealthy kinsman whose name is
Boaz, and when Ruth goes to glean in his field Boaz
shows an interest in her. Naomi goes to great lengths
to encourage the acquaintance, which ripens into
love. The result is the marriage of the two, signifying
a closer union between the awakening spiritual sense
(Ruth) and the consciousness that abides in the
spiritual (Boaz). Charles Fillmore states that Boaz
represents:

The cheerful willingness, promptness, and quickness
of action, also richness and power of thought, and strength
of character, that when established in substance (Bethlehem) and allied with the love of the natural man (Ruth)
open the way for the birth of the Christ into consciousness
(M.D. 130).

By following our highest impulse (as Ruth did)
we come to know peace, happiness, and such an en-
richment of the spiritual consciousness that seeds
are planted which ripen into the Christ realization.
The birth of Obed, the son of Ruth and Boaz, symbolizes this. Obed became the grandfather of David,
a type of Christ.

The Book of Jonah (written about 350 B.C.)

The Book of Jonah is a didactic work with a
time setting in the period of the Assyrian empire,
prior to the destruction of Nineveh in 612 B.C. It

was written as a protest against racial and religious exclusiveness. The Jews were wont to believe that they were God's chosen people and deserved special favors from Him. The story of Jonah brings out the truth that all men are dear to the Almighty and that His mercy is ever extended to those who turn to Him.

As a practical spiritual lesson, The Book of Jonah is exceedingly valuable. Jonah is a type of individual who lives close to God and thus is receptive to divine direction but exceedingly stern in his conception of righteousness. Charles Fillmore states that Jonah represents:

> That prophetic state of mind which, if used without divine love, fixes man in bondage to belief in a law of cause and effect wherein error sowing cannot be redeemed or forgiven (M.D. 361).

Jonah was commissioned by the Lord to go to Nineveh, in Assyria, to "cry against it; for their wickedness is come up before me" (Jonah 1:2). If the Ninevites did not repent their great city was to be destroyed. This was an exceedingly disagreeable duty for the prophet, because he had reason to hate the Assyrians, who had inflicted great distress upon the Hebrews. Moreover, according to Jonah's point of view, they were godless men and had no right to be saved.

We are like Jonah when we have developed spiritually to the point of receiving divine guidance and are prompted to perform a service for one who, from our point of view, is not only a sinner but has proved to be an enemy. We are therefore reluctant to extend a helping hand. We are prone to feel that justice should be done; that is, that the wrongdoer should pay the penalty for his transgressions.

Our reaction to the sinner should be entirely different. "When error effects are revealed to one by the prophetic faculty of mind, which is open to receive the outpicturing of thought causes, one should fearlessly tear away the error and immediately proclaim the saving Truth, in the spirit of forgiving love. 'Jonah' must be glad and must rejoice in omnipotent good" (M.D. 361). Jonah should have been grateful for the opportunity to help his fellow man; instead, he attempted to evade his duty, "even as you and I."

The prophet fled to Joppa and took a ship to Tarshish. In disobeying our highest leading, no matter what excuse we make, we bring trouble upon ourselves. A great storm arose on the sea and Jonah was tossed from the ship. The condition we think will save us often proves our undoing. We, too, are swallowed by a "great fish" (Jonah 1:17), meaning that we fall into a disastrous state of affairs. Then, like Jonah, we are exceedingly repentant and cry to the Lord.

God, who is love, always gives us another chance. We, having learned at least part of our lesson—the futility of attempting to resist our revealed duty—resolve to perform it. Jonah proceeded immediately to Nineveh. He met his enemy and rendered the service designed by the Lord.

We also may act with the wrong spirit. The good

deed without the good motive behind it adds no jewel to our crown. Jonah was still certain that the Ninevites should perish. He had no conception of the spiritual teaching "Love your enemies and pray for them that persecute you" (Matt. 5:44). When the Jonah state of consciousness rules in us, we may do our job capably, but as love and mercy are absent from our hearts, we are disappointed in the outcome of our work.

Anyone with a strong sense of justice, as viewed from the human plane of thought, is likely to fall into Jonah's dilemma. His preaching was successful. The Ninevites, from the king down, repented so effectively that their city was saved. If we help a person against our personal will, he may receive great benefit but we go away empty-handed, dismayed that things did not turn out as we thought they should.

Jonah was angry at this unexpected turn of events. He sulked under the gourd that the Lord, in His mercy, had caused to grow to protect Jonah from the sun. The gourd pleased Jonah, as we are pleased when any good is manifested for us, though we may be reluctant to give God the credit. However, when we fail to give Him credit we also fail to retain the good. A worm destroyed the gourd. Jonah, who had not yet recovered from his disappointment that the Ninevites had been saved, found the destruction of the gourd quite too much. Bitterness and self-pity overcame him. He "fainted, and requested for himself that he might die" (Jonah 4:8). Whereupon the Lord reminded him that he showed pity for the gourd though he was without compassion for the people of a great city.

We feel a certain amount of sympathy for Jonah, as perhaps all of us have been in his shoes at times. Through an experience similar to his, which we are quite likely to have, may we learn this: "The true prophet must see as God sees—that only the good is true. Evil and all its effects pass away when men repent, and the compassion and love of God should always be proclaimed to the sinner. By asking, the suffering one may obtain forgiveness; and he who is soul-sick may receive the divine compassion" (M.D. 362). As we willingly share God's forgiving love with others, even those who in our eyes are unworthy, we receive our own freedom and joy.

The Book of Job was also written during this period, sometime between 400 and 350 B.C., and will be discussed in detail in the last chapter.

The messages of the prophet Joel came during the last years of Persian rule over Judea.

Joel (350 B.C.)

Joel was a native of Jerusalem and began his ministry at a time when a great plague of locusts had caused much suffering among his people because of the destruction of crops. To Joel this was a sign of divine judgment, and he declared that the Jews could be delivered only if they repented:

Rend your heart, and not your garments, and turn unto Jehovah your God; for he is gracious and merciful, slow to anger, and abundant in lovingkindness, and repenteth him of the evil (Joel 2:13).

Repentance, Joel insisted, should not be a mere outward act but a real change of heart. When this comes about we are again in tune with God, or good. "Joel bespeaks the I AM in dominion in the individual" (M.D. 355), that in us which calls us to God in contriteness of heart. Then only can we receive His cleansing.

It is Joel who hears the Lord's promise to restore all that has been lost through man's failure to unify himself with the Lord:

> And I will restore to you the years that the locust hath eaten . . . And ye shall eat in plenty and be satisfied, and shall praise the name of Jehovah your God, that hath dealt wondrously with you; and my people shall never be put to shame (Joel 2:25).

This is one of those wonderful promises that thrill us with new hope. "The years that the locust hath eaten" symbolizes the periods of our lives that seemed devoid of good. They are the times when trouble reigned in mind or body or outer conditions, and we almost believed that a malicious fate stalked our path, a fate over which we had no more control than a farmer has over a swarm of locusts that suddenly destroy his crop. Or those years may be the periods when we lagged spiritually, when our prayers were unanswered and we could not get close to our Father-God. In the mortal consciousness, nothing of the past can be changed, but when we rise to the spiritual, God can give so much to the present moment that it seems to fill even the empty days of the past also. "I will restore to you the years

that the locust hath eaten." If we turn to Him, there
is no longer any belief in loss. Rather we shall eat
in plenty and be satisfied and praise the name of Jehovah, our God. The outer fullness comes quickly
when there is the inner sense of completeness.

Beginning with verse 28 of chapter 2, The Book
of Joel becomes apocalyptic in character and deals
with what shall come after man is purified. We can
almost hear the joy in the prophet's voice as he uttered these words of the Lord:

> And it shall come to pass afterward, that I will pour
> out my Spirit upon all flesh; and your sons and your
> daughters shall prophesy, your old men shall dream dreams,
> and your young men shall see visions. . . . And I will
> show wonders in the heavens and in the earth . . . And it
> shall come to pass, that whosoever shall call on the name
> of Jehovah shall be delivered (Joel 2:28-32).

Greek Conquest (333 B.C.)

Persia continued to govern Palestine until 333
B.C., when Darius III, the last of the Persian
kings, was defeated by Alexander the Great at Issus.
Greece had been slowly rising to power; several of
the Persian kings had attempted to subdue her, but
without success. When Alexander of Macedonia assumed control of the Greek armies, the fate of
Persia was sealed. Within a few years, Alexander
had taken the lands as far as the Indus River in
India, and when he died at the age of thirty-three,
still longing for more worlds to conquer, his mighty
empire was the greatest in extent the world had ever
known.

Alexander was the enthusiastic champion of Hellenism and was determined to spread Greek culture throughout his enormous domain. He founded a number of Greek cities, the most important of which was Alexandria in Egypt. The spread of Greek ideas throughout his empire was the first sharp clash between Eastern and Western civilizations, and it exerted a profound influence on the world's culture. It met a resistant wall in Judaism.

Hellenism was a social movement, kindling patriotism, inspiring decadent people into a higher and broader type of life, preaching the brilliant, joyous, virile, artistic use of ability and strength. Judaism was a religious faith, sturdy, serious, believing in moral ideas and issues and cultivating holiness. To a Jew the Greek seemed light-hearted, unmoral, and often godless: to a Greek the Jew seemed intolerant, narrow, and stupid, concerned with trifles. The greatest difference was that the Greek ideal was at heart a selfish one; the Hebrew ideal was at heart sacrificial. Each, however, needed the other (History of the Hebrews, Frank Knight Sanders).

In God's great scheme of things nothing occurs by chance, and that which seems a misfortune is often a blessing in disguise. Historically, the shift of power from East to West was to prove beneficial to civilization. Religiously, the injection of Greek ideas was to broaden the rigid though fine spiritual teachings of Judaism. When considered from the standpoint of our spiritual unfoldment, this change tends to balance the consciousness. In the beginning of our search for God we may be a bit too serious and pay undue attention to an exact outer obedience to the divine law as it is revealed to us, overlooking the fact that religion should encompass the whole of man, the inner spirit as well as the human self. Gradually we come into a greater sense of freedom and discover that joy is as necessary as righteousness. A happy combination of the two is found in Jesus, who, while He said that every jot or tittle of the law must be obeyed, also asserted, "These things have I spoken unto you, that my joy may be in you, and *that* your joy may be made full" (John 15:11).

When Alexander the Great died in 323 B.C., his empire was partitioned among three of his generals. Antigonus, who received the northwest section, was defeated within a few years. Western Asia was divided between Ptolemy, who secured Egypt and Palestine, and Seleucus of Syria, who retained the remainder. Egyptian rule over Palestine was mild, and the Jews prospered and were content.

Since the eighth century the Jews had been settling in various parts of the Mediterranean world outside of Palestine itself, and they came to be called the Jews of the Dispersion or Diaspora. On the whole, they were far more receptive to Greek ideas than were the Palestinian Jews. They spoke Greek, and as there was a large community of them in Alexandria, Egypt, they undertook to translate the Hebrew Scriptures into Greek. This translation is called the Septuagint and was begun about the middle of the third century. The Greek translation served Jews living outside Palestine, and it also made the Hebrew sacred writings available to

Gentiles. It was the Septuagint that was used much later by the converts to Christianity.

The Jews in Palestine formed the bedrock of conservatism and during the latter years of the third century B.C. they produced two books belonging to the wisdom literature of the Bible, The Proverbs and Ecclesiastes. The Proverbs is a collection of maxims that had been written over a period of at least six centuries. The book is divided into five main sections dealing with (1) the value of wisdom, chapters 1-9; (2) contrast between righteousness and wickedness, chapters 10-19; (3) general warnings and instructions, chapters 20-29; (4) the words of Agur, chapter 30; (5) the words of King Lemuel, closing with the description of and tribute to a virtuous woman, chapter 31. The Proverbs contains much of practical wisdom and many beautiful statements of Truth, one of the finest of which is the admonition:

> Trust in Jehovah with all thy heart,
> And lean not upon thine own understanding:
> In all thy ways acknowledge him,
> And he will direct thy paths
>
> (Prov. 3:5, 6).

Ecclesiastes, the Greek equivalent of the Hebrew name Koheleth, is a most thought-provoking book for it asks and answers the question, "Is life worth living?" The unknown author is a Jewish philosopher who impersonates Solomon, renowned for his wisdom. He calls himself "the Preacher" (Eccles. 1:1).

Koheleth gives his verdict of life before he recounts his experiences, saying flatly, "all is vanity" (Eccles. 1:2) (the word vanity is used in the sense of empty or futile). The reason for his pessimistic outlook is based on his various frustrations. He has endeavored to discover the true value of life but finds only "vanity and vexation of spirit" (Eccles. 2:11). His initial quest was for worldly wisdom and knowledge, only to discover "in much wisdom is much grief; and he that increaseth knowledge increaseth sorrow" (Eccles. 1:18). His search for happiness through pleasure ends in emptiness. He accumulates wealth but to what purpose? He may not live to enjoy it, and who is worthy to inherit his possessions? The doing of great works is likewise unavailing. All about him he sees oppression and cruelty. Life is filled with uncertainty, day follows night in a monotonous routine, and "there is no new thing under the sun" (Eccles. 1:9). Death ends all for saint and sinner alike. He believes there is a superior Being even though it is difficult to reconcile his belief in a good God with the apparent inequalities and failures of life.

The views of Koheleth reflect those of a person looking at life from the human plane, alone, and invariably the only inference to be drawn is a discouraging one. Such a state of consciousness comes to many a thinking individual. There are times when we all ask, "What profit hath man of all his labor?" (Eccles. 1:3). But there is something in us, as there was in Koheleth, that will not permit life's final curtain to be drawn at this point. The very fact that we perceive there is a God is the starting point for a saner concept of human existence. Into the mind comes the realization, "God made man upright" (Eccles. 7:29). It is man himself who has "sought out many inventions" (Eccles. 7:29). There must be a way to bring meaning and purpose to living. Gradually a superior wisdom begins to operate in the mind. There is something worth while to be done. Learn to be charitable: "Cast thy bread upon the waters; for thou shalt find it after many days" (Eccles. 11:1). Rejoice in life itself, for there is much of pleasantness in it. Be moral: "Therefore remove sorrow from thy heart, and put away evil from thy flesh" (Eccles. 11:10). It is well to "Remember also thy Creator in the days of thy youth, before the evil days come and the years draw nigh, when thou shalt say, I have no pleasure in them" (Eccles. 12:1).

The sage conclusion of Koheleth to the whole matter of living is, "Fear God, and keep his commandments; for this is the whole *duty* of man" (Eccles. 12:13). He is assured that we are under the government of a beneficent and just God who "will bring every work into judgment, with every hidden thing, whether it be good, or whether it be evil" (Eccles. 12:14). Ecclesiastes represents:

Experience. Experience preaches very effectively; the fruit of experience is the most impressive sermon in life. Experience teaches us that it is impossible to find satisfaction and true lasting joy in sensual, earthly pleasures and in self-seeking. The only way to gain the realities of life that satisfy both soul and body is to turn within to God and become unified consciously with Him (M.D. 181).

CHAPTER XIX

Intertestamental Period

Part II
Daniel; Esther

IN 198 B.C. Antiochus III (the Great) of Syria gained control over Palestine by defeating the Egyptians. This change proved disastrous for the Jews. They seethed with resentment under the harsh rule of Syria. When Antiochus IV Epiphanes, grandson of Antiochus III, came to the throne in 175 B.C., added troubles began for Judea.

The new king was determined to Hellenize his empire completely. During the first years of his reign he developed a hatred for the racial and religious tenacity of the Jewish people, and in 168 B.C. he attacked Jerusalem, looted the Temple, and stationed a garrison of soldiers in the city who deliberately desecrated the sacred precinct. The ownership or even reading of copies of the Law was forbidden on pain of death. The Jews were not permitted to worship at Temple or synagogue and were compelled to sacrifice swine's flesh to the Greek god Zeus on their own Temple altar. These demands at first frightened and then infuriated them. They saw all too clearly that the Syrian monarch was bent on exterminating Judaism. In fear some of the Jews complied with the exactions imposed, but many thousands fled to the desert rather than do so. The Syrian soldiers made a thorough search of all Judea, forcing each group of people that they found to submit or be killed.

A Jewish priest named Mattathias, of the house of Hasmon, retired to the little town of Modein some twenty miles northwest of Jerusalem, hoping to escape the Syrians. When they arrived and attempted to compel him to sacrifice to Zeus, Mattathias slew the Syrian commander and made his escape. This act inaugurated a new chapter in the history of the Jews, for it started what is known as the Maccabean revolt.

Mattathias had five sons. Together they gathered many followers and retreated to the central mountains of Judea to prepare for war. Within a year or two Mattathias died and his second son Judas assumed leadership of the rebel forces. Judas was given the name Maccabaeus, meaning "the hammer." He was a patriotic and energetic leader and, though the Syrian army greatly outnumbered his, Judas won victory after victory. Finally he was able to take Jerusalem. He cleansed the Temple, tore down the altar to Zeus and built a new altar to Jehovah, refurnished the House of God, and re-established the regular order of worship. In commemoration of this, the annual Feast of Dedication or Lights was instituted.

In 161 B.C. Judas was slain in battle and Jonathan, his brother, became leader of the Jewish forces. Jonathan was not able to throw off the Syrian yoke completely but, due to dissension in the court of Syria, he won one concession after another until he was the recognized head of Judea in civil and religious matters.

It was during the time of struggle with Syria that The Book of Daniel was written.

The Book of Daniel (written about 165 B.C.)

The scene of the book is laid in the days of the Babylonian captivity (586-536 B.C.). Its action centers around Daniel, a Jew who rose to a position of power in Babylonia. The unknown author named his book after the Daniel whom Jewish tradition affirmed to be one of the three men specifically distinguished for righteousness, the others being Noah and Job. Daniel was renowned for wisdom also.

The purpose of the book was to give inspiration and courage to the Jews in their war with Syria. Hard pressed as they were, they needed to be reminded that their God was so mighty, so loving that if they would trust in Him, nothing that Antiochus Epiphanes could do would defeat them.

The Book of Daniel is divided into two parts, the first six chapters containing stories of Daniel and his three companions, Shadrach, Meshach, and Abednego. No accounts of faith recorded in the Bible or elsewhere are told more thrillingly and dramatically. They are universal and timeless in their appeal; therefore, they encourage us in our own spiritual unfoldment.

Daniel and his friends, like all the other characters in Scripture, represent states of consciousness. When those belonging to the spiritual plane rule in us, we can overcome seemingly insurmountable obstacles. Daniel signifies:

Spiritual judgment. . . . conscious integrity. He typifies the clear, penetrating insight of Spirit. Daniel humbled himself in the presence of the universal Mind, and thereby opened his understanding and made himself receptive to the cosmic consciousness (M.D. 164).

Shadrach, Meshach, and Abed-nego stand for an understanding of God as "love, mercy, goodness, and the channel of all power, wisdom, Truth to the manifest man" (M.D. 587).

The opening chapter of Daniel shows why the four Jews were superior to the Babylonians. Daniel and his friends lived at the royal court. Nebuchadnezzar, the king, represents the "human will backing itself up by the human intellect" (M.D. 474). When the will is entrenched in intellectual learning, its full attention is given to material consideration. The king and his court are thus symbolic of a material way of living, and Daniel and his companions symbolize that which is spiritual.

The Jews were urged to share the king's food, but Daniel "purposed in his heart that he would not defile himself with the king's dainties, nor with the wine which he drank" (Dan. 1:8). In a spiritual sense to eat and drink means to appropriate in consciousness. Thus Daniel's refusal to take the king's food and wine signifies his unwillingness to partake of the consciousness of materiality. It is only as we cultivate purity of mind and heart by adhering strictly to the spiritual that we can open the way to function on the higher levels of consciousness.

Daniel was able to interpret dreams and visions. He made known the king's dream of the great figure (Daniel 2), the vision of the mighty tree (Daniel 4), and the handwriting on the wall at the feast of Belshazzar (Daniel 5). There is only one Mind in which we, as individuals, have consciousness. When we are attuned to this Mind we have the ability to fathom what are mysteries to those in material thought. Daniel always turned quickly to the Lord when asked for an interpretation, freely admitting that of himself he could not discern the meaning. Today we do not spend time analyzing dreams as such, but we often need light on certain experiences, as well as to understand our own or another's motives. We can discover whatever is necessary for us to know if we will turn to the inner source of wisdom. When the revelation comes, may we, as Daniel did, pour out our thanksgiving to the Lord. We may even use Daniel's prayer of praise:

> Blessed be the name of God for ever and ever; for wisdom and might are his. . . . he revealeth the deep and secret things; he knoweth what is in the darkness, and the light dwelleth with him (Dan. 2:20, 22).

As a reward for his outstanding wisdom Nebuchadnezzar "made Daniel great, and gave him many great gifts, and made him to rule over the whole province of Babylon, and to be chief governor over all the wise men of Babylon" (Dan. 2:48). At Daniel's request Shadrach, Meshach, and Abed-nego also were given positions of authority.

When we function in the spiritual consciousness, we have superhuman power that attracts outer recognition, and we desire to share our good with others.

The two dramatic incidents of Shadrach, Meshach, and Abed-nego in the fiery furnace, and Daniel in the lions' den, have many points in common. It seems as if the writer of the book, knowing full well that the Jews needed fortitude and resoluteness in their struggle with Syria, sought to impress upon them as forcibly as possible the fact that their God was all-powerful and could and would protect and sustain them if they trusted in Him. Antiochus Epiphanes was no more dangerous than a burning furnace or a den of lions, and those who served and believed in the Lord were delivered without harm.

Today these great stories of faith thrill us. Some of the conditions we meet are harrowing indeed, and as we listen to the accounts of Daniel and his friends our hearts are lifted in faith and our lagging courage is restored. May we be brought to the realization so effectively expressed by Paul, who said:

Nay, in all these things we are more than conquerors through him that loved us. For I am persuaded, that neither death, nor life, nor angels, nor principalities, nor things present, nor things to come, nor powers, nor height, nor depth, nor any other creature, shall be able to separate us from the love of God (Rom. 8:37-39).

The Babylonians were idol worshipers, and Nebuchadnezzar had made an image of gold, and demanded that all his subjects worship it. When the King's decree went forth over the land the three

Jews, Shadrach, Meshach, and Abed-nego, refused to obey. They were brought into the King's presence and threatened with death. "If ye worship not, ye shall be cast the same hour into the midst of a burning fiery furnace; and who is that god that shall deliver you out of my hands?" (Dan. 3:15).

This is a test as to whether we shall worship God or mammon. Mammon (the golden image) will reward us if we bow down to him. His power is great, judged externally, and we are sorely tempted to accede to his demand. But when spiritual thoughts (the three Jews) rule in consciousness, the demand is rejected. Shadrach, Meshach, and Abed-nego vowed they would not worship the image of gold. Moreover they said, "Our God whom we serve is able to deliver us from the burning fiery furnace; and he will deliver us out of thy hand, O king" (Dan. 3:17).

These are brave words and reveal a substantial faith. Only those who are faithful to God understand His power. Many who acknowledge Him and ask for protection do not serve Him. We really serve whatever god we think of and are attuned to. The god of pleasure has many worshipers; devoted followers of the god of money are legion. Some even make a god of worry by giving it the substance of their thought day and night. Have we served the true God in mind, word, and deed? If so, we know Him and believe that He can save.

"The burning fiery furnace" stands for a severe trial of any sort. Can we plunge into the very midst of it, or do we turn back at its very brink, sacrificing our integrity rather than face it? What happened to the three friends is the revelation of what happens to us when we hold fast to the God whom we serve.

When Nebuchadnezzar looked into the furnace the next morning he was amazed to see not only the three men but a fourth, and the aspect of the fourth was "like a son of the gods" (Dan. 3:25). This fourth man is the angel of His presence, the protecting power of God that preserves us through all evil. It is "the consciousness of one's I AM in its spiritual unity with God" (M.D. 587). This realization can be so powerful that others are aware of it. Truly, "When thou walkest through the fire, thou shalt not be burned, neither shall the flame kindle upon thee" (Isa. 43:2).

As Shadrach, Meshach, and Abed-nego stepped from the furnace they were so completely unharmed that not a hair of their heads was singed, their coats were not burned, nor was there even the smell of smoke about them. This would indicate that we can pass through a difficult situation without hurt if we maintain a steadfast trust.

Daniel was to undergo a supreme test also. It took place after Babylonia had been conquered by the Persians. The Darius mentioned in The Book of Daniel is unknown to history, as Cyrus was the first of the Persian kings. However, the author of Daniel was far less interested in history than in the actions of God and man.

According to the Biblical account, Darius had set Daniel over the other ministers of state in the kingdom and thus aroused their jealousy. They influenced the King to decree that no one was to petition any save the King for a period of thirty days, else he would be cast into a den of lions. Knowing that Daniel prayed daily to his God, they had made this plot to destroy him. Spying on Daniel, they found him making supplication before the Lord, and word of this was relayed to the King. The King sincerely repented of his rash command, as Daniel was a favorite of his. But upon being reminded that nothing could alter the law of the Medes and Persians, Darius ordered that Daniel be cast into the lions' den, saying to him, "Thy God whom thou servest continually, he will deliver thee" (Dan. 6:16).

The next morning Darius looked into the den and called. Daniel promptly answered, "My God hath sent his angel, and hath shut the lions' mouths, and they have not hurt me" (Dan. 6:22).

That which would annihilate us (the lions of disease, poverty, sorrow) is powerless before a consciousness superbly poised in faith. How did Daniel acquire such faith? We are told that he prayed three times a day before a window opened "toward Jerusalem" (Dan. 6:10). This sentence is a fine definition of true prayer; "toward Jerusalem" signfies a mind turned to the spiritual. We should pray, not as we so often do with attention focused on the difficulty, but with our thought centered on God, the solver of any human problem. The number 3 represents the trinity of man's being: Spirit, soul, and body. To pray three times a day, therefore, signifies the whole man caught up in a spiritual cycle of thought. When we make a practice of scientific prayer and sustain the awareness of God's presence throughout a trial (lions' den), the result is perfect freedom. "So Daniel was taken up out of the den, and no manner of hurt was found upon him" (Dan. 6:23).

The Book of Daniel is the chief apocalypse of the Old Testament. Chapters 7-12 consist of a series of visions predicting the events of the four centuries from the Babylonian captivity (Daniel's day) to the Maccabean War (the time the book was written). The visions relate in symbolic language the destruction of the four earthly kingdoms, Babylonia, Media, Persia, and Greece, and prophesy that the "little horn" (Antiochus Epiphanes) is also doomed (Dan. 8:9). The tyrant is to fall and that soon. Then will come the reign of the heavenly kingdom.

The idea of life after death is brought out clearly in Hebrew writings for the first time in the final chapter of the book:

And many of them that sleep in the dust of the earth shall awake, some to everlasting life, and some to shame and everlasting contempt. And they that are wise shall shine as the brightness of the firmament; and they that turn many to righteousness as the stars for ever and ever (Dan. 12:2, 3).

Life is indeed everlasting, and when a body is lost through death, the real self (which is immortal) continues existence. Whatever consciousness we develop in life on earth is retained. "They that are wise shall shine as the brightness of the firmament," meaning that those who have attained spiritual consciousness shall know freedom and joy in eternal life. Those governed by the sense mind find the next existence filled with frustration and unhappiness. In time they, too, shall find their God.

The period of the Maccabean revolt marks the time of the writing of The Book of Esther and the final editing of the Psalter, or The Psalms.

The Book of Esther (written about 150 B.C.)

The scene of the narrative is laid in the days of Persian rule about 485 B.C. The king called Ahasuerus (which was a title rather than a name) refers to Xerxes. The book relates the story of how the Jews in Persia were threatened with destruction by one Haman, who was jealous of the positions occupied by the Jewish queen Esther and her uncle Mordecai, and how the Jews were saved by Esther's bravery and cleverness. Written in a period of intense nationalism, it emphasizes Jewish resentment of foreign rule and tends to arouse a spirit of revenge toward those who would persecute their race. The book served to popularize the joyous festival of Purim. Its spiritual interpretation has many helpful ideas to convey to us.

Esther and Mordecai were Jews, and they represent spiritual qualities in the individual. Esther signifies spiritual love and Mordecai signifies "a spiritual power working within each soul for its full re-demption" (M.D. 459). The two other prominent characters, Ahasuerus and Haman, stand for phases of the sense consciousness. Ahasuerus symbolizes the will, proud and dominated by ambition, and Haman signifies "the activity of the phase of the carnal con-sciousness in man that gives itself up particularly to working against man's religious thoughts and tendencies" (M.D. 251).

The story depicts the conflict between the higher and baser qualities of mind, showing by means of the main events of the narrative how the spiritual (Esther) finally overcomes the carnal (Haman).

Esther, the Jewess, marries Ahasuerus, king of Persia. Her uncle Mordecai arouses the enmity of Haman, the King's chief minister, by refusing to bow down to him. Haman, unable to avenge him-self on Mordecai personally, conceives the plan of having Ahasuerus issue an edict to put all the Jews in the kingdom to death by telling him that they are disloyal subjects. The carnal consciousness is in opposition to the spiritual. It is jealous for power and strives to eliminate all that stands in the way of its unwholesome desires.

Mordecai sends word to Esther and instructs her to appear before the King to plead for mercy for the Jews. The Queen is exceedingly reluctant to do this; for Ahasuerus has not summoned her, and to force her way into his presence might mean death. She has to make the choice between selfish and selfless action. This is a choice that we are all called upon to make many times. Shall we protect the human self at the expense of righteousness? When divine love (Esther) is active in consciousness we choose unselfish service.

Esther sends word to Mordecai to have the Jews fast for three days. Sustained by the spiritual (Jews), Esther also fasts (denies all personal considerations). This must be done before we can hope to influence the strong human will (Ahasuerus). When we are determined to follow our higher leading (as Esther was) we are willing to let results be what they may. "So will I go in unto the king . . . and if I perish, I perish" (Esth. 4:16). This is equivalent to our saying, "I will do what I know to be right, regardless of the consequences."

When the choice is made and spiritual love triumphs, we have the courage to do what is before us. Esther goes into the King's presence. As the will is approached by love, it extends a welcome. Ahasuerus holds out his golden scepter, which Esther touches. The King then asks what she wants and promises it will be granted, even to half of his kingdom. Under the domination of the carnal consciousness (Haman), the will is cruel (typified by the signing of a decree for the destruction of the Jews), but it can always be won over by divine love. If we understand this, we need not fear the strong will of any person who seems bent on injuring us.

Esther is exceedingly clever. She does not reveal her real request at the time. It is not wise to act too hastily, especially when great issues are at stake.

Esther merely asks that Ahasuerus and Haman attend a banquet which she will prepare for them. The King consents willingly, and Haman is delighted to be so honored. In the meantime, Haman orders gallows to be prepared, on which he plans to hang Mordecai. The carnal consciousness is flattered by attention and speeds up its nefarious plan to be rid of its foe without regard to justice. However, error thought is self-destructive; it prepares its own grave. At the banquet Esther tells the king of the plot against her and her people, naming Haman as the instigator. Ahasuerus is so infuriated that he gives orders for Haman to be hanged. And so Haman is hanged on the very gallows he had had built for Mordecai. "And Esther set Mordecai over the house of Haman" (Esth. 8:2).

This is another Bible story that tells us very effectively that victory is assured whenever we act in accordance with our highest revelation of righteousness. The lesson is repeated innumerable times in the Scriptures. In unifying ourselves with what is godly, we become open channels through which God can move to bring His good into manifestation. Our part is to be faithful to Him. "Only be strong and very courageous, to observe to do according to all the law . . . for then thou shalt make thy way prosperous, and then thou shalt have good success" (Josh. 1:7, 8).

The date 150 B.C. or shortly thereafter is generally given for the completion of the Psalter. This book belongs to the poetic literature of the Bible and is the noblest and undoubtedly the most beloved book of prayer for Jew and Christian alike. The Psalter is similar to The Proverbs in that it is a compilation, the one hundred and fifty psalms having been written over a period of hundreds of years beginning with the time of David.

Maccabean Kingdom (143-63 B.C.)

Simon, the last remaining brother of the Hasmonean leaders, succeeded Jonathan. Simon was a wise and noble sovereign, and the year 143 B.C. marked the beginning of real Jewish independence, which was to last for eighty years, or until 63 B.C. Simon was followed by his son John Hyrcanus, a strong ruler who did much to enlarge the power and prestige of his kingdom.

When Hyrcanus died his eldest son Aristobulus I came to the throne, to be followed a year later by his brother Alexander Jannaeus. Jannaeus was the least religious and most unscrupulous of the Hasmonean kings. His was a despotic rule of twenty-six years, the influence of which was only partially offset by the more constructive reign of his widow Alexandra. At her death, after a reign of nine years, her two sons Hyrcanus II and Aristobulus II contended for the throne. This resulted in a vicious civil war. Hyrcanus allied himself with Antipater, the governor of Idumea, who was to play an important part in Jewish history.

In an effort to settle the contest for the throne, both Hyrcanus and Aristobulus sought to enlist the aid of Rome. Pompey, the Roman general, was in Syria at the time, and when approached by parties representing the contending factions, Pompey simply annexed the entire territory, making Judea a province of the Roman Empire. Thus, in the spring of 63 B.C., the Maccabean kingdom came to an end and with it Jewish independence.

Roman Rule (63-4 B.C.)

Pompey reinstated Hyrcanus II as high priest and administrator with the title of ethnarch, and appointed Antipater (the Idumean) as adviser to Hyrcanus. Antipater became the real power in Judea. The wily Idumean managed to keep Roman favor even after Julius Caesar deposed Pompey, and was made governor of Judea. He appointed one of his sons, Phasael, governor of Jerusalem, and another, Herod, governor of Galilee.

Herod, like his father, was a clever statesman, and when Antony came to power in Rome, Herod was made king of all Judea. He came to be known as Herod the Great. He was an efficient administrator but utterly ruthless. The Jews despised him. To have a member of hated Idumea (formerly Edom) as their king caused them to spit at the very mention of his name.

Herod tried to win Jewish favor by rebuilding the Temple, making it a magnificent structure. The Jews were duly proud of it, though they continued to detest the man responsible for it. They knew he built it not for love of God but that Herod's name might gain renown. In his later years, Herod became completely degenerate, and the Jews sighed with relief when he died in 4 B.C.

Earlier in that same year, or perhaps in 6 B.C., an event occurred that was to shake the foundations of the world and result in fulfilling the noblest ideals of the Hebrew prophets. Jesus Christ was born in the little town of Bethlehem.

CHAPTER XX

Job

THE BOOK OF JOB is a suitable finale to these lessons, for it is a masterpiece. Its theme is lofty, its language superb; it has, moreover, a vital spiritual message for every person on the path of spiritual enlightenment. Job blazed the trail from self-righteousness to spiritual righteousness, from the human to the divine level of goodness. May we, like Job, hear the voice of the Lord. Only His voice can drown out the sounds of the world of sense, which alone are responsible for every ill.

The book belongs to the wisdom literature of the Bible and is of late composition, fourth century B.C. It is a product of profound spiritual thinking. Based on an old folk tale of Job, a patriarch of Edom, the work is a dramatic poem set in a frame of prose. The Prologue and Epilogue are written in prose, and the main sections, chapters 3-42:6, are poetry. These sections comprise the longest sustained poetical composition in the Bible.

The five parts of the book are:

1. Prologue—Conversation between Jehovah and Satan (1-2)
2. Three cycles of discourses—Job and his friends (3-31)
3. Elihu sections—Elihu's address to Job and his friends (32-37)
4. Speeches of Jehovah—Resulting in Job's submission (38-42:6)

5. Epilogue—Job's reward (42:7-16)

The book raises a question that has been asked by countless millions: "Why do the righteous suffer?" Job does not answer it, and the reader must draw his own conclusion. The Prologue implies that suffering is a test of character. Job's friends are firm in their conviction that suffering is always punishment for sin. Elihu agrees with the friends that suffering is closely connected with sin, but points to the disciplinary purpose of suffering, which is a warning to turn to God. A metaphysical interpretation offers a better solution. All men suffer, even those who are righteous from the human point of view, until their eyes are opened to the omnipresence, omnipotence, and omniscience of God. We must move from even the highest plane of human consciousness to a realization of that supreme good which is God, and give ourselves fully to Him. In the story of Job we discern the steps that will enable us to make this transition and rise from suffering to wholeness of mind, body, and affairs.

The cast of characters of this mighty drama includes:

Job	A godly man seeking a spiritual answer to the problem of suffering.
Satan	The bringer of distress to Job.
Eliphaz	A religious dogmatist who is spiritually wise in his own sight.
Bildad	A religious dogmatist of the superficial kind.
Zophar	A religious dogmatist who presumes

to know the ways of God.

Elihu   Who turns Job's attention to the Almighty.

Jehovah   Who awakens Job to a realization of His omnipotence.

1—*Prologue*
Chapters 1-2

The narrative begins with a description of Job, a man "perfect and upright, and one that feared God, and turned away from evil" (1:1). He has great wealth and a goodly household, a wife, seven sons, and three daughters. "This man was the greatest of all the children of the east" (1:3). Job's goodness is so outstanding that when the heavenly beings present themselves to Jehovah, He says to Satan, "Hast thou considered my servant Job? for there is none like him in the earth" (1:8). Satan insinuates that Job is pious because he has been blessed in all ways: "But put forth thy hand now, and touch all that he hath, and he will renounce thee to thy face" (1:11).

Whereupon Jehovah gives Satan permission to deprive Job of his possessions, and immediately all is lost to the patriarch. The Sabeans steal his oxen and asses, fire burns his servants and his sheep, the Chaldeans steal his camels, and a great wind blows down the house where his sons and daughters are feasting and kills them.

Then Job arose, and rent his robe, and shaved his head, and fell down upon the ground, and worshipped: and he said, Naked came I out of my mother's womb, and naked shall I return thither: Jehovah gave, and Jehovah hath taken away; blessed be the name of Jehovah (1:20, 21).

The Lord rejoices that Job still praises Him. Satan hints that the catastrophe has touched only Job's possessions but that if Job himself were afflicted, he would renounce Jehovah. "And Jehovah said unto Satan, Behold, he is in thy hand; only spare his life" (2:6). Job is then smitten "with sore boils from the sole of his foot unto his crown" (2:7). Sinking down upon an ash heap, deprived of health as well as possessions, Job is reviled by his wife, who urges him to "renounce God, and die" (2:9). This Job refuses to do, asking, "Shall we receive good at the hand of God, and shall we not receive evil?" (2:10).

Three of Job's friends, Eliphaz the Temanite, Bildad the Shuhite, and Zophar the Naamathite, hear of his adversity and come to comfort him. They do not recognize their friend at once, so changed is he in appearance and circumstances. Rending their robes and sprinkling dust upon their heads, they sit down with him on the ground seven days and seven nights without speaking, "for they saw that his grief was very great" (2:13).

2—Discourses between Job and his friends
Chapters 3-31

Job finally breaks the silence. He has refused to curse God but curses instead the day he was born. The annals of literature contain no deeper cry of misery and despair. Job begins with the bitter words:

Let the day perish wherein I was born,
And the night which said, There is a man-child conceived.
Let that day be darkness;
Let not God from above seek for it,
Neither let the light shine upon it

(3:3, 4).

Seeing the depths of Job's anguish, Eliphaz, the oldest of the friends, begins to speak. He reminds Job that he (Job) has strengthened others and should not faint now that misfortune has overtaken him. Eliphaz firmly believes that Job's state is the result of wrongdoing.

According as I have seen, they that plow iniquity,
And sow trouble, reap the same

(4:8).

His counsel to Job is,

Behold, happy is the man whom God correcteth:
Therefore despise not thou the chastening of the Almighty

(5:17).

Job's calamity is heavy upon him and he resents the counsel of Eliphaz, saying, "To him that is ready to faint kindness *should be showed* from his friend" (6:14). He asks for instruction, not blame:

Teach me, and I will hold my peace;
And cause me to understand wherein I have erred

(6:24).

Bildad the Shuhite is the next friend to speak. What rash folly is in Job's words. "Doth God pervert justice?" (8:3). Bildad then continues:

If thou wert pure and upright:
Surely now he would awake for thee,

And make the habitation of thy righteousness prosperous
                                                    (8:6).

Job agrees that God's power is great and it is impossible to answer Him. But God is capricious and unkind,

> For he breaketh me with a tempest,
> And multiplieth my wounds without cause.
> He will not suffer me to take my breath,
> But filleth me with bitterness
>   (9:17, 18).

Zophar, the third friend and speaker, rebukes Job for his challenge of God's justice, asserting that righteousness and piety bring light and peace, and that the wicked should repent:

If thou set thy heart aright,
And stretch out thy hands toward him;
If iniquity be in thy hand, put it far away,
And let not unrighteousness dwell in thy tents.
Surely then shalt thou lift up thy face without spot;
Yea, thou shalt be stedfast, and shalt not fear;
For thou shalt forget thy misery;
Thou shalt remember it as waters that are passed away.
And *thy* life shall be clearer than the noonday;
Though there be darkness, it shall be as the morning
                                                    (11:13-20).

When Job answers Zophar he seems to be somewhat disgusted with everything in general and his "comforters" in particular. He grows sarcastic:

> No doubt but ye are the people,
> And wisdom shall die with you.
> But I have understanding as well as you;
> I am not inferior to you
>   (12:2, 3).

The three friends apparently had the kindest motive, but they could not understand why Job was made to suffer so much, unless he had incurred Jehovah's wrath by sinning. Being religious dogmatists, the friends had nothing except traditional ideas of religion to offer. Charles Fillmore states that they represent "accusations against self and attempted self-justifications of the outer or personal consciousness" (M.D. 355). They all say many true things, and their words antagonize Job because he does not believe he has erred. When a person is in trouble it is not helpful to him to be told that he brought it upon himself. What Job needed was a new and totally different point of view. He needed to be able to look at his situation not with mortal but with spiritual eyes. Jesus taught that we must be "born anew" (John 3:3); that is, we must come into an awareness of God as the one reality and be able to interpret conditions in the light of the spiritual. As long as we ponder and fret over our troubles, wondering why we have them, feeling a sense of self-pity or injustice, we are seeing them with limited human sight, and no healing can come about. We need a fresh outlook, a new birth in consciousness. Job's friends were incapable of helping him do this. They had many religious concepts but no real spiritual understanding. They condemned Job for what they considered his transgressions, but they did not have the insight to point out to him that his dire experience of the moment was opportunity to transform his whole outlook on life.

Job accused his friends of looking with contempt upon his misfortunes. They might, he said, defend the Lord with misleading statements, but he (Job) was not to be deceived. He knew man's lot was a hard one:

> Man, that is born of a woman,
> Is of few days, and full of trouble.
> He cometh forth like a flower, and is cut down:
> He fleeth also as a shadow, and continueth not
>
> (14:1, 2).

In the second series of discourses (chapters 15-21) Job's friends continue the old theme that the wicked man "travaileth." Job reproaches them for their heartlessness. If they were in his condition, he would strengthen and comfort them. He feels himself forsaken by both God and man; "My days are past, my purposes are broken off" (17:11).

Bildad speaks again, criticizing Job for rejecting his friends' counsel. He assures Job that reverses in this life and dishonor after death shall be the lot of the wicked. Job contends that God is unjust:

> Behold, I cry out of wrong, but I am not heard:
> I cry for help, but there is no justice.
> He hath walled up my way that I cannot pass,
> And hath set darkness in my path
>
> (19:7, 8).

Suddenly rising from the depths of despair, Job exclaims:

> But as for me I know that my Redeemer liveth,
> And at last he will stand up upon the earth:
> And after my skin, *even* this *body,* is destroyed,

Then without my flesh shall I see God
(19:25, 26).

In the third cycle of discourses (chapters 22-31)
Job's comforters deal with his specific sins. Job is
accused of taking a man's garment for a trifling debt,
of neglecting the poor and appeasing the rich, of op-
pressing widows and fatherless children. Eliphaz ad-
vises:

Acquaint now thyself with him, and be at peace:
Thereby good shall come unto thee. . . .
If thou return to the Almighty, thou shalt be built up,
If thou put away unrighteousness far from thy tents.
And lay thou *thy* treasure in the dust . . .
And the Almighty will be thy treasure,
And precious silver unto thee.
For then shalt thou delight thyself in the Almighty,
And shalt lift up thy face unto God.
Thou shalt make thy prayer unto him, and he will hear thee;
And thou shalt pay thy vows.
Thou shalt also decree a thing, and it shall be established
        unto thee;
And light shall shine upon thy ways
(22:21-28).

This is one of the noblest passages in the whole
of the Scriptures, and had it been said after Job's
mind had been cleansed of fear and doubt, he could
have profited by it, as we so often do. He could not,
however, acquaint himself with God until he had
learned to be still and quiet the human thought that
was raging in his mind.

Evidently Eliphaz's words have some effect upon
Job, for he says he would gladly turn to the Lord but
that he cannot find Him:

Oh that I knew where I might find him!
That I might come even to his seat!
I would set my cause in order before him,
And fill my mouth with arguments. . . .
Behold, I go forward, but he is not *there;*
And backward, but I cannot perceive him;
On the left hand, when he doth work, but I cannot behold
     him;
He hideth himself on the right hand, that I cannot see him.
But he knoweth the way that I take;
When he hath tried me, I shall come forth as gold
                                    (23:3-10).

Bildad takes up the conversation, asserting that God is great and not a mere worm; Job should not presume to question the Almighty.

Job replies that in spite of God's treatment of him, he still affirms his innocence. He knows, as well as his friends, that there is no real profit in wickedness, but he no longer argues with them nor questions the Lord. His mind reverts to days that have passed, and he longs for their return:

Oh that I were as in the months of old,
As in the days when God watched over me;
When his lamp shined upon my head,
And by his light I walked through darkness
                              (29:2, 3).

Throughout the discourses with his friends, Job was unable to understand wherein he had transgressed sufficiently to bring such adversity upon himself. Job's idea of righteousness was not high enough. Measured by human standards, he was an upright and devout man, but inwardly he was fear-

ful and terribly self-righteous. These were the root
of his misfortunes. None of his friends discerned
this, and Job reveled in bitterness, condemnation of
the Lord, self-pity, and self-defense. Occasionally he
rose to great faith,

> Behold, he will slay me; I have no hope:
> Nevertheless I will maintain my ways before him
> (13:15),

only to lose faith and return to poignant questioning.

Toward the end of Job's conversation with his
friends, he recalls the years of his prosperity and happiness, contrasting them with his present humiliation
and wretchedness. He refutes the charge that he has
treated others unjustly and affirms the integrity of
his entire life:

Oh that I had one to hear me!
(Lo, here is my signature, let the Almighty answer me)
And *that I had* the indictment which mine adversary hath
    written!
Surely I would carry it upon my shoulder;
I would bind it unto me as a crown:
I would declare unto him the number of my steps;
As a prince would I go near unto him

> (31:35-37).

After this the friends can say nothing more. They
have served the purpose of letting Job "talk out" his
troubles. The vicious cycle of thought and destructive emotion has been broken by Job's challenge,
"Let the Almighty answer me." Elihu the Buzite begins to speak, leading Job to the point of being able
to hear Jehovah's answer.

Up to this point Job has looked at his afflictions as due to outer causes. He has not yet really looked within himself. This is necessary if we are to come into a higher understanding. On our part there must be a willingness to be directed by Elihu (Holy Spirit). He will tell us how to turn our attention from self to Spirit.

3—*Elihu Sections*
Chapters 32-37

Elihu is a young man who, having listened to Job and his friends, is filled with wrath against Job "because he justified himself rather than God" (32:2), and against Eliphaz, Bildad, and Zophar because "they had found no answer, and yet had condemned Job" (32:3). Now he, Elihu, has something to say. He contends that though Job and his friends are older, the old are not always wise. Rather,

There is a spirit in man,
And the breath of the Almighty giveth them understanding
(32:8).

Elihu has a more spiritual view of the situation because he has a higher conception of God. He represents "the Holy Spirit. The name Elihu also signifies the recognition by man that his true inner self is Spirit" (M.D. 191).

Elihu has heard Job declare his innocence against the accusations of his friends and is aware of Job's inability to find out why the Lord has afflicted him:

Behold, I will answer thee, in this thou art not just;
For God is greater than man.

> Why dost thou strive against him,
> For that he giveth not account of any of his matters?
> > (33:12, 13).

Job, according to Elihu, did wrong in arguing and defending himself.

> > Job speaketh without knowledge,
> > And his words are without wisdom
> > > (34:35).

Is his righteousness more than God's? He should turn to the Lord and await His answer: "The cause is before him, and thou waitest for him!" (35:14).

Elihu's words help to free Job from a complete attachment to himself and his woes. Bound by the chains of self-righteousness, Job was unable to get a higher perspective. Elihu suggests that Job be humble, for "He regardeth not any that are wise of heart" (37:24). Finally Job is willing to "stand still, and consider the wondrous works of God" (37:14). His mind is quiet and directed to Him. Job's life has reached its climax. In such an attitude of receptivity, no one can fail to receive inspiration (hear the voice of the Lord). We all need to be still and listen.

4—*Speeches of Jehovah and Job's submission*
Chapters 38-42:6

> Then Jehovah answered Job out of the whirlwind, and said,
> Who is this that darkeneth counsel
> By words without knowledge?
> Gird up now thy loins like a man;
> For I will demand of thee, and declare thou unto me
> > (38:1-3).

Jehovah's words are impressive and majestic. They consist of a series of questions designed to bring Job to a realization of his feebleness as compared with the might of Jehovah, of his ignorance as contrasted with the wisdom of the Lord:

Where wast thou when I laid the foundations of the earth?
Declare, if thou hast understanding.
Who determined the measures thereof, if thou knowest?
Or who stretched the line upon it?
Whereupon were the foundations thereof fastened?
Or who laid the corner-stone thereof,
When the morning stars sang together,
And all the sons of God shouted for joy?

(38:4-7).

On and on stretch the questions unanswerable by man. Where were you when the seas broke forth, when the day was established? Have you entered into the springs of the sea, or have the gates of death been revealed to you?

Where is the way to the dwelling of light?
And as for darkness, where is the place thereof?
(38:19).

Where are snow and hail reserved? How is the light parted, and the east wind scattered upon the earth? What can you say about the rain, the dew, the waters that freeze?

Canst thou bind the cluster of the Pleiades,
Or loose the bands of Orion?

(38:31).

Do you understand the ordinances of the heavens, or can you lift up the voice of the clouds? Can you

feed the beasts of the field and the fowl of the air?
Do you know how they function and where each can
find his rightful place? He who would argue with
the Almighty, let him reply.

Then Job answered Jehovah, and said,
Behold, I am of small account; what shall I answer thee?
I lay my hand upon my mouth

(40:3, 4).

The Lord continues by describing two impressive creations, the behemoth and the leviathan. The
behemoth is generally identified as the hippopota-
mus, and the leviathan as the crocodile.

Throughout the discussions with his friends, Job
has been questioning the justice of God because of
his affliction. Job is now convinced that God is a
power mightier than he conceived, and he is willing
to yield completely to the Most High:

I know that thou canst do all things,
And that no purpose of thine can be restrained.
Who is this that hideth counsel without knowledge?
Therefore have I uttered that which I understood not,
Things too wonderful for me, which I knew not.
Hear, I beseech thee, and I will speak;
I will demand of thee, and declare thou unto me.
I had heard of thee by the hearing of the ear;
But now mine eye seeth thee:
Wherefore I abhor *myself*,
And repent in dust and ashes

(42:2-6).

In the end Job did exactly what his friends urged:
he repented. But it was not in the way nor for the
reason they advanced. They counseled repentance

for sins of which Job was unconscious or which he denied having committed. The word repent has two meanings. One of them is to be penitent or regretful of one's conduct. This is the type of repentance advocated by Job's friends and the thing Job refused to do. The second meaning of repent is to change the mind, and repentance signifies a turning from the mortal to the spiritual. Job's repentance came after he listened to Jehovah and understood why he should lose personal concepts and take on spiritual ones. This is really putting off the "old man" as Paul terms it, and putting on the "new man, that after God hath been created in righteousness and holiness of truth" (Eph. 4:24). Such repentance is necessary on the part of each of us. No one has yet attained perfection, and though we may not be aware of specific sin, an outer condition of limitation is proof of deviation from divine law or a limited understanding of that law. "Who can discern *his* errors?" Our prayer should often be, "Clear thou me from hidden *faults*" (Psalms 19:12).

We all retain much that separates us from the wholeness implanted in our spiritual nature. Only a spiritual quickening, such as the divine voice that Job heard, reveals it. Job could have received this revelation at the beginning of his trial had his mind not been so concerned with his own distress. So can we, but like Job, we are apt to build self-defenses that close our ears to all but the fury of our own misery. When we eventually exhaust ourselves, we call on the Lord and in the stillness of our hearts we hear Him and come to a realization of His infinite presence, wisdom, and power moving throughout the universe as well as in us.

None of the lofty concepts presented by his friends seeped into Job's consciousness, for it was enclosed by the stone wall of self-pity. When he moved from human reason and personal complaint, a higher idea, as given by Elihu, took root in Job's mind. This prepared the way for the Spirit of truth to be heard, and when the revelation came, Job turned from self to Self, repenting of his sin of self-righteousness.

Spiritually Job represents:

The transition of man from personal, formal righteousness, which is the basis of self-righteousness, to a true inner change of heart and an entrance into the real Christ righteousness, which deals with the very thoughts and intents of the innermost consciousness instead of merely setting right a few outer acts (M.D. 354).

5—*Epilogue*
Chapter 42:7-16

Jehovah's wrath is kindled against the friends, "for ye have not spoken of me the thing that is right" (42:7). However, Job prays for them, "And Jehovah turned the captivity of Job, when he prayed for his friends: and Jehovah gave Job twice as much as he had before" (42:10).

Job's mind and heart were utterly right with the Lord, "So Jehovah blessed the latter end of Job more than his beginning" (42:12). Do we not have more of every good as a result of reaching a higher level of consciousness, of knowing that God *is* and that from Him comes every perfect gift?

May we, like Job, discover why the righteous suffer. Human goodness is not sufficient to protect us from "the slings and arrows of outrageous fortune." We must learn to lose ourselves in God and be able to say, with Paul, "that *life* which I now live in the flesh I live in faith" (Gal. 2:20). Such is the only righteousness that lifts us to the heights and lets the peace and power of the Almighty within come into full expression.

Epilogue

J ESUS CAME into the complex religious and political situation that existed in Judea at the beginning of the first century A.D. His birth was unheralded by the Jews, who were waiting with longing and keen anticipation for the Messiah, whose coming had been foretold by their great prophets. There was indeed no room for Him "in the inn" (Luke 2:7), yet He was to bring to fruitage the profound and noble verities proclaimed by the spiritual seers of His race. He was to carry on and give wider scope and meaning to the words of Moses, "Hear, O Israel: the LORD our God *is* one LORD" (Deut. 6:4 A.V.). He was to remember and use the counsel of His great predecessor, "Ye shall seek Jehovah thy God, and thou shalt find him, when thou searchest after him with all thy heart and with all thy soul" (Deut. 4:29). He was to teach obedience to God's command as given through Isaiah, "Look unto me, and be ye saved, all the ends of the earth; for I am God, and there is none else" (Isa. 45:22). He was to fulfill the prophecy of Isaiah, "For unto us a child is born, unto us a son is given; and the government shall be upon his shoulder: and his name shall be called Wonderful, Counsellor, Mighty God, Everlasting Father, Prince of Peace" (Isa. 9:6).

The search for God is the sublime adventure of each man, and this the Bible records. In the Old Testament are given the steps to be taken in preparing the mind and heart for still greater truths to be found in the New Testament. From the time

281

of Abraham to that of Jesus was a long period, approximately two thousand years by human reckoning. This brings to mind that the overcoming of the deficiencies of the human consciousness requires time— time to let faith, perseverance, and love for God and man permeate the whole man. Throughout our period of preparation may we remember that the righteous are never forsaken, that the light of Truth illumines our way. May we rest assured that obedience to the Highest brings all manner of good into our lives. May we, like David, be inspired to worship the Lord "in the beauty of holiness" (I Chron. 16:29 A.V.). All this establishes a foundation in consciousness upon which we can build an awareness of the ever-present kingdom of heaven. Surely the fulfillment of the supreme truth that man is made in the image and likeness of God comes in the triumphant declaration of Jesus Christ, "I and the Father are one" (John 10:30).

At Moses' command Aaron blessed the Children of Israel, whose spiritual descendants we are, with words that are ours to accept this day:

"The LORD bless thee, and keep thee:
    The LORD make his face shine upon thee,
        and be gracious unto thee:
    The LORD lift up his countenance upon thee,
        and give thee peace."

INDEX

INDEX

consciousness, abides in spiritual, 234; background of, 92; balance of, 241; carnal, 258, 259; Christ, 90; cleansed of errors, 163; closed to spiritual guidance, 155; confused state of, 188, 198; cosmic, 59; David state of, 111, 115; destructive attitudes of, 63, 127; environment a picture of, 35; error states of, 132, 141; faculty of order in, 221; fearful state of, 117; foundation in, 282; higher levels of, 67, 250, 279-280; higher thoughts active in, 216; high place in, 39, 69, 121; I AM of, 135; Jehu, 142; Jeremiah state of, 177; Jonah state of, 237; love active in, 258; man's power to identify, 21-22; more important than action, 221; mortal, 15, 66, 158, 202, 239; need to change, 148, 189, 197; Nehemiah state of, 223; new, 33, 76; new birth in, 269; of Immanuel, 108; of Job, 279; of materiality, 249; of peace, 223; of the masses, 173; Omri state of, 127; one phase of, 136; overcoming deficiencies of, 282; permeated with divine ideas, 27; physical and mental phase of, 44; poised in faith, 254; prayerful, 101; predominant thought in, 133; purifying of, 64; renewal of, 208; represented by Temple, 121; ridding of destructive thoughts, 130; rising in, 214-215; safeguarding against destructive forces, 222; sensuous desire in, 114; Spirit triumphant in, 202; spiritual, 86, 109, 125, 129, 144, 155,

162, 164, 169, 178, 188, 205, 206, 207, 210, 212, 216, 223, 225, 234, 251, 252, 256; spiritual defenses in, 179; state(s) of, 9, 29, 54, 67, 99, 148, 244, 248; steadfast, 128; strength established in, 196; symbolized by Ezekiel, 190; to be sustained, 228; Truth active in, 175; unredeemed elements of, 61, 87; unregenerate state of, 229; upright, 191
consequences, 258
conservation, 243
consolation, 197
contempt, 270
contriteness, 239
co-operation, 178, 208
Corinthians, 228
corruption, 149, 153
cosmos, 69, 153
counsel, 267, 270, 281
courage, 66, 147, 160, 177, 194, 204, 224, 230, 248, 251, 258
courts, 149
covenant, 30, 45, 227; new, 184
covetousness, 73, 88
creation, two accounts of, 14-15; six days of, 16; steps in, 15-18
Creator, 15, 71, 110
creatures, living, 190
credit, to God, 237
creed, 168
creeping things, 18
crisis, financial, 179
criticism, 72
cruel(ty), 244, 258
curse, 266
customs, religious, 151
Cyrus, 200, 203, 204, 209, 253

daily bread, 66
Damascus, 162
Damocles, 193
Dan, 48, 126

that lead to, 190; would
annihilate us, 254
soul, 19, 233, 255
sowing, 209
speckled and spotted animals, 49
spies, 75, 83-85
Spirit, attuned to, 98; breathes
life into us, 195; co-operation
with, 111; guidance of, 85;
harmony with, 96; intellect
functioning apart from, 125;
in trinity, 255; life of, 215;
light of, 191; never dies, 143;
of truth, 62, 123, 147, 170,
279; power of, 212; return
to, 205, 274; search for, 203,
222; vitalizes and restores,
144
spirit, religion of, 177
spiritual, ability to interpret
conditions in light of, 269;
allegiance to, 162; ascendance
over human, 51, 257, 258;
drawing closer to, 149; for-
saking, 183; mind tuned to,
254, 278; precedence of material over, 148, 207; removed
from, 190; rising to, 239;
symbolized by Daniel, 249
spiritual-minded people, 168,
203
standard(s), ethical and moral,
211; human, 272; spiritual,
148, 152
steadfast(ness), 187, 201, 222
stealing, 150, 265
still(ness), 98, 271, 278
still, small voice, 138
storm, 236
strength(en), 76, 96, 101, 132,
145, 159, 163, 166, 168, 181,
182, 190, 195, 196, 222, 228,
267, 270
study, 221
submission, 263
substance, overcoming lack of,
179; spiritual, 232

success, price of, 226
suffering, cause of, 26, 160;
for others, 193, 201; reason
for, 264, 269, 280; vicarious,
201
surety, sense of, 137
surrender, 138, 185
symbolism, 190, 191-192
Syria(ns), 82, 123, 127, 128,
129, 138, 141, 145, 156, 242,
246, 247, 248, 251, 261
system, in religious life, 221;
orthodox, 232; religious, 217

Tabernacle, 73, 74
talk, 224
Tamar, 116
Tarshish, 236
taxes, 122, 149, 227
teach, ability to, 176
teacher(s), 147, 160, 183, 193,
205, 222, 232
teaching(s), spiritual, 237, 241
Tekoa, 148, 225
Temple, 118, 120-121, 125, 126,
163, 164, 165, 168, 172, 173,
178, 180, 185, 203, 204, 205,
206, 207, 208, 212, 213, 215,
217, 219, 220, 228, 229, 231,
246, 247, 261
temptation(s), 24-25, 50-51, 88,
150, 208, 221
tenacity, 246
Ten Commandments, 67, 69-73
Terah, 34, 44
test, of Abraham, 42; of Daniel,
253-255; of man, 139, 252,
264
thanksgiving 132, 250
theology, 201
thievery, 72
thigh, 50
thirst, 66, 199
Thomas, 117
thought(s), adverse, 136, 224;
centered on God, 254; de-
structive, 214, 273; error, 259;

About the Author

Elizabeth Sand Turner was born on July 5, 1897, in Nashville, Tennessee. Raised an Episcopalian, she became interested in Unity when her mother, Elizabeth Pierce Sand, visited Unity School in Kansas City in 1910 and received a healing.

Elizabeth Turner's mother founded the Unity center in Nashville in 1916. While Turner attended occasionally, she did not take an active role in the church. She worked with the Nashville, Chattanooga, and St. Louis Railway and, for a time, became business manager and secretary for a lecturer on practical psychology.

A visit by Unity lecturer Francis Gable in 1932 motivated Elizabeth to explore Unity again. In the fall of that year she enrolled in the Unity Correspondence School and became the spiritual leader of the Nashville center in 1933. In 1934 she was licensed a Unity teacher and then ordained as a minister in July 1936.

Elizabeth served as minister at the Unity Center of Christianity in Nashville until 1945. In 1946 she became a field lecturer for Unity School and in the fall of that year was made educational director of the ministerial training school. She worked there until 1955. In 1958 she moved to Fort Lauderdale, Florida, and served as minister at the Unity church there until August 1966. Elizabeth Sand Turner made her transition on May 1, 1979.

A lover of music and of the Bible, Elizabeth

studied the Bible at Peabody College in Nashville. She is now best known for her trilogy of books which metaphysically interprets the Bible: *Let There Be Light* (1954), *Your Hope of Glory* (1959), and *Be Ye Transformed* (1969). *Let There Be Light* is dedicated to her mother, Elizabeth Pierce Sand, "who first inspired in me a love for God."

Printed U.S.A.

22-2387-5M-3-96